Parental Influences

Parental Influences

The Importance of Authority
in Child Development

William Bacon

Edited by Paul Dennis Sporer

GAVRINIS PRESS

ANZA PUBLISHING, Chester, NY 10918
Gavrinis Press is an imprint of Anza Publishing
Copyright © 2005 by Anza Publishing

This work is a new, unabridged edition of *Parental Influence, Authority, And Instruction: Their Power and Importance* by Rev. William Bacon, originally published by Miller, Orton & Mulligan in 1856.

Library of Congress Cataloguing-in-Publication Data
Bacon, William, 1789-1863.
   Parental influences / William Bacon; editor, Paul D. Sporer.
     p.   cm.
   Includes index.
   ISBN 1-932490-11-6 (hardcover : acid-free paper)
   1. Child rearing—Religious aspects—Christianity.
   2. Parenting—Religious aspects—Christianity.
I. Sporer, Paul D. II. Title.
BV4529.B284 2004
248.8'45–dc22   2004015460

Visit AnzaPublishing.com for more information on outstanding authors and titles. Please support our efforts to restore great literature to a place of prominence in our culture.

⊚ This book is printed on acid-free paper.

ISBN 1-932490-11-6 (hardcover)

Contents

Editor's Preface

William Bacon attempts to cover a wide range of issues that parents must confront in helping their children become responsible Christians. His book takes the controversial position that corporeal punishment, although it should be avoided, must be used when children do not readily accept other forms of inducement to obey parental authority. Not everyone will agree with its premises, but it provides critical information on the justification for physical discipline.

Bacon believed in the concept of a household "absolute government"; the child must understand that ultimate law and justice rest with the parents, and refusal of requests cannot be tolerated. Bacon also believed in what we today would call behaviorism: that the human child, like other creatures, can only attain a productive life through guidance that is clear, steadfast, and goal-orientated. The natural tendency in man is to disobey, and if his tendencies are not checked, he will fall into moral ruin.

Parental Influences was published originally by Miller, Orton & Mulligan in 1856 to a favorable reception. The work received such comments as: "judiciously and ably handled", "eminently practical", "judicious treatment", "full of sound and important ideas", "valuable and timely and plainspoken instruction". Clearly, there were many pastors who approved of Bacon's approach to the issue of parental authority.

We have preserved the entire text, making only the necessary corrections, and on a few occasions rewording a statement. The formatting of the book was made more modern, and we have also added an index.

PAUL DENNIS SPORER

Romans v. 12.

*"Wherefore, as by one man sin entered into
the world, and death by sin; and so death
passed upon all men, for that all have sinned."*

Exodus xx. 5, 6.

*"I, the Lord thy God, am a jealous God,
visiting the iniquity of the fathers upon the
children unto the third and fourth generation
of them that hate me; and showing mercy
unto thousands of them that love me and
keep my commandments."*

Genesis xviii. 19.

*"For I know him, that he will command
his children and his household after him,
and they shall keep the way of the Lord, to
do justice and judgment, that the Lord may
bring upon Abraham that which he has
spoken of him."*

Lecture 1

Importance of Parental Training

These passages are stepping-stones that will lead us to a right position as to the duty of "training up our children in the way they should go." The first passage teaches us, that in consequence of the sin of Adam, all his posterity are born with a propensity to sin; and, therefore, that the chief aim of parents should be to repress this propensity in their children, in order to secure their salvation.

The second passage teaches, that there is an important connection between every parent and his posterity; that is, that, somehow, God visits the sins of parents upon their children even to the fourth generation, and shows mercy to thousands (supposed to mean thousands of generations[1]) of those that love and obey him. Not that he literally *punishes* children for the *sin,* or *rewards* them for the *obedience* of their parents. The passage teaches only, that the consequences of a parent's conduct will reach his posterity. And this fact is held out to him as an inducement to "cease to do evil" and "learn to do well." The consideration is, that sin will injure, and obedience benefit, both ourselves and our posterity. Hence, the outbreathing of divine benevolence: "Oh, that there were such an heart in them that they would fear me, and keep my commandments always, that it might be well with them and with their children forever."[2]

But how do the consequences of the parent's conduct affect his posterity? Mostly, through their moral training. While the sin of Adam reaches all his posterity through native *depravity,* the sins of other parents reach theirs through *parental nurture.* Impenitent parents, instead of restraining and repressing the evil inclinations of their children, are doing much to foster and confirm them—doing it by example—doing it by allowing, and even by approving, of their wrong feelings and conduct — no, by prompting them to these things; while, on the other hand, faithful believing parents will train their children "in the way they should go", the way of repentance, faith, and salvation. This is confirmed by the last passage of the text.

"For I know him, (Abraham,) that he will command his children and his household after him, and they shall keep the way of the Lord to do justice and judgment; that the Lord may bring upon Abraham that which he hath spoken of him." The thing spoken of him was, that "In him all the families of the earth should be blessed."[3] Here we are told not only why the promise was made to him, but how it was to be fulfilled. It was by his training his household to "keep the way of the Lord." This passage alludes, no doubt, to the atonement of Christ. But it points, mainly, to an important means by which the blessings of this atonement are to be attained; that is, to right moral training. It is true, that Abraham could have commanded but few generations of his descendants to follow him; but it is to be understood, that those whom he did train would bring up their children as he brought them, and that each successive generation would do the same.[4]

This means of grace is not only the first in order of appointment and practice, but first in importance and efficacy. It has neither been annulled nor superseded; nor has its necessity or efficacy been in the least abated. Says the author of "Parental Duties,": "God has established a connection between parental fidelity and extensive blessings to the church; and it were not going too far to affirm, that the piety of the household is a means more honored than any other, for raising up, and continuing on earth, a holy seed." (p. 144.)

Although Sarah is not named in the last passage of the text, she is virtually included in it, as Eve is in the first. In scripture, as in law, the interests, rights, and duties of the wife are merged in those of her husband. In these respects, they are "one flesh." And though the mother's name is often omitted, where parental interests are spoken of, yet, in other passages, she is mentioned most emphatically; as in the following: "Honor thy father and thy *mother.*" "My son, hear the instructions of thy father, and forsake not the law of thy mother." "My son, keep thy father's commandment, and forsake not the law of thy mother." "The eye that mocketh at his father, and despiseth to obey his mother, the ravens of the valley shall pick it out, and the young eagles shall eat it."[5]

It is a fact, too, that in many respects the mother's agency in Christian nurture is more important than that of the father. This is emphatically true in the earlier stages of childhood. For then she is with them much more than he, and, consequently, has more occasion to restrain and instruct them. And as they are more dependent on her, and receive more kind attentions from her, she has the better opportunity to win their affection and confidence, and, thereby, their obedience. Besides, she has those warmer, finer sensibilities which give her, in this respect, still greater advantage.

And, on several accounts, early childhood is a very important portion of human existence. Although many regard the first six or nine months of the child's life as almost a blank, both as to its mind and morals, the truth is far otherwise. It will be found, on observation, that the character of the future man is more deeply and durably stamped during that portion of childhood which may be called the mother's dynasty, than during any equal portion of its after life. Yes; the mother gives shape to the little moral nucleus, and thus decides, in a great measure, the form of the final mass.

If we look into history, sacred or profane, we shall find much to confirm us as to the importance of a mother's agency in forming the moral character of men. Look at the mother of Moses, whose early education of her son was the evident means of saving him from being overborne by the corrupting influence of the schools of Egypt, and of the court of Pharaoh, and thus, of making him the deliverer of Israel, and the lawgiver of that people. Look at Hannah, whose training of her son Samuel fitted him to receive, even in his child-hood, the messages of the Most High, and afterward, to be a judge of Israel. Look at Elizabeth, mother of John the Baptist, and at Eunice, mother of Timothy. Look at Nonna, mother of Nazianzem, and at Anthusa, mother of Chrysostom. Look at the mothers of Augustin, of John Newton, and of many others, whose early instructions were the means of preparing their sons for pious and useful careers, or of reclaiming them after they had gone far off in the ways of the profligate. Compare the mother of Solomon with the mother of Ahaziah, the mother of Washington with the mother of Napoleon, and the mother of John Quincy Adams with the mother of Lord Byron.

It is often said that extraordinary men have extraordinary mothers, and that this happens according to "the vascular system," or that physical law by which "like produces like." But much, if not all, of this correspondence may be referred to the mother's influence on her child after its birth, yet so early after it, as to be generally over-looked. In confirmation of this, look at the maternal training of Sir William Jones, Bishop Hall, Cowper, Doddridge, Cecil, Swartz, Brainard, Edwards, and Dwight; and to these many other names might be added.

The younger a child is, the finer and more flexible, the softer and more impressible, must be its mental and moral constitutions. It is alive to everything that addresses its senses, and the feeblest in-fluences may be stamping durable impressions upon it. A process of moral daguerreotyping is thus constantly carried on in the soul of the young child. And though the characters thus impressed are not now legible, still, they are there, and will show themselves more and more in future life. They are like the characters written with invisible ink, and which become legible only as they are exposed to light or heat. How important, then, is that part of the child's life when it is mostly under the eyes and actions of its mother; and, therefore, how important that the mother's influence should be of the right kind. For, how correct the opinion of Napoleon, that *"a man is what his mother makes him."*

And it is very important that the father and mother should be perfectly harmonious in the training of their children, lest what the one does the other should more than undo. In all their concerns they need to be not only "one flesh," but *one spirit.* But in the government of their household, this union is emphatically needful. They should, therefore, consult together more on this than on any other of their household affairs; and if they do disagree in opinion on the subject, they should be careful never to let their children see it.

It is particularly injurious for one parent to interfere with the other, in the *government* of a child. It tends to ruin the authority of both parents, and thus to spoil all their children. I know a rich, but wretched family, which owed its wretchedness to the fact, that when the father attempted to correct his eldest child, the mother snatched it from him, and ran into another room with it. Thinking it useless, he resolved never again to attempt the government of his family. And he kept his word, to their social, if not to their eternal undoing.

Professor Lindley gives a striking instance of this error, as follows: "I was guest in a family, respected for wealth, and for their pretensions to high life. The mistress of the house had in her lap a child about a year old. She had occasion, in the discharge of her maternal duties, to cross its inclinations; and the child became angry, and resisted, with its might, the mother's will. The mother, in a calm, but very prompt and decided manner, subdued its passion, and produced a quiet and calm submission. But the father soon took the child in his arms, clasped it to his bosom, and condoled with it, in such language as this: 'Did mother slap my poor little son? She will not do it anymore. Poor son, his heart is almost broken. Give me blows in my hand, to strike mother. Shake your fist at her.'

"The mother remonstrated with him, not to ruin the child that she loved. But the father vindicated his conduct, by saying, 'Wait till the child gets old enough to know his duty, and then he will need no correction.' His degraded wife silently withdrew, to weep in secret over the ruin which she foresaw was likely to overtake her children, and over the contempt into which she would be likely to be brought at some future day, when her children would be old enough to trample down her pious authority." *(Infant Philosophy, pp. 27, 28.)*

Few parents, perhaps, are guilty of interference as gross as this; yet many, I fear, are approaching too near to it. How often does a child hear one parent chiding the other for punishing or reproving it? And what is this, but teaching the child to justify itself, and to disregard parental authority? Nor is it enough to abstain from interference. Mere silence will be often understood as a token of disapprobation; and if the disapprobation be but *felt,* the child will be sure to read it in the looks and actions of its parent. And this will prolong its stubbornness, and, perhaps, prevent its submission; for it is natural to it, when corrected by one parent, to look for sympathy to the other.

This is illustrated by what occurred with two fathers of my acquaintance, the one an elder, the other a minister of the Presbyterian church. "I had," said the elder, "a sore trial when I first enforced obedience on my eldest daughter. She remained a long while stubborn under the rod. At length I saw she was looking to her mother for pity. I had, therefore, to request my wife either to leave the room, or to use the rod herself. She, therefore, gave her a few blows, when she cheerfully submitted."

"And," said the minister, "just such a thing occurred in the government of my eldest daughter. My wife began to punish our little one for disobedience, and I was inwardly sorry for it, thinking the child was too young to be corrected. She continued obstinate for a long while. At length my wife saw the reason was, that she was looking to me for sympathy. She therefore said, 'Mr. S., I shall not be able to conquer this child unless you, also, apply the rod.' Whereupon, I gave her a few strokes, when she yielded."

Parents should strive in various ways to increase, instead of diminishing each other's authority. For instance: when one gives a command that is not immediately obeyed, the other should repeat it, and with additional sternness; or should express astonishment or grief that the child did not obey this commandment at once "What! will you disobey your mother?" (or father, as the case may be.) This should be the sincere and earnest expression of one parent, when the other is not instantly obeyed.

It may be more especially the duty of the husband to command and correct the household. But if he neglects to do so, it is the duty of the wife to make up the deficiency. And either should exercise authority, as the occasion requires, for instance, while the other is absent or occupied. It is the understanding of some families, that the father shall direct the sons, and the mother the daughters. But for the exact fulfillment of this arrangement, I see neither revelation nor reason. If either parent sees an order or a chastisement needed, it is his or her, duty to give it. Nor should fathers or mothers allow a child to understand, that they have relinquished their authority over any portion of their households.

It is especially unwise in one parent to call on the other to govern the children. How weak in a mother to say, "Father, do speak to this child—he won't let me dress him;" or to say to the child, "If you do not behave, I will tell your father of you." And how weak and undignified for a father to say, as many have been heard to say, "Mother, why don't you keep these children still; I can't hear myself think." Both parents should be, and show themselves to be, perfectly adequate and equal in parental authority.

It is most evident, from the word and providence of God, that he has committed the moral training of children to their own fathers and mothers. And in this arrangement there is more wisdom than infidels allow, or theologians are wont to appreciate. For, as they are so much of their time necessarily with their children, they have the more opportunity to "train them up in the way they should go." And filial affection gives them a vast advantage in discharging this duty; while in their parental love they find the strongest motives to be faithful. I cannot, therefore, but consider it most unwise, as well as unauthorized, to commit this duty to "sponsors,"[6] as some churches are doing; or to "committees," as some classes of infidels are doing. For these substitutes can have neither the opportunities, advantages, nor inducements that parents have, to "bring up these children in the nurture and admonition of the Lord." What an abortive attempt is this, then, to improve on the wisdom of God; an attempt the more to be regretted, as it tends to lessen parental regard to the obligations and encouragements of the Family or Abrahamic Covenant.

It appears to me that parental nurture, considered as a means of grace, has long been sadly undervalued, both by parents and by the church of Christ. The preaching of the gospel seems mostly relied upon as a means of salvation. But this is plied upon the heart after it is sadly "hardened through the deceitfulness of sin;" whereas parental training takes the heart in hand while it is comparatively tender, and more easily molded. It is true, that neither of these means of grace will be effectual, except as it is rendered so by the influence of the Spirit of God. But is there not more hope of securing this effectual influence for the young, than for those who have long been resisting and grieving it? And is there not ample encouragement in the Abrahamic Covenant, that if we strive faithfully to "train up our children in the way they should go," the Spirit will be given to render us successful?

I may overrate this subject; but it seems to me that none is more important, either to the country or the church, and none needs more to be insisted on at the present day. Three dangers now threaten us: *insubordination, infidelity,* and *the influx of an ignorant and corrupt population.* But, if all our Christian professors were sufficiently excited to examine and to do this duty, our land would be safe. As ours is a republican government, it must be self-sustained. We have not, like monarchies, a strong military force for sustaining law. It is the more needful, then, that our citizens have such a habit of *self-government* as shall make us a law-abiding people. And they that obey their parents first, will be most likely to obey their reason, then their rulers, afterward. Self-control, then, should be cultivated in the nursery. The most turbulent and outbreaking of our citizens, and those most ready to mingle in our mobs, are those the least taught and governed at home. But while right parental training is especially needful here, it is more neglected, I fear, than in Scotland and England, and in some parts of Ireland and Germany — owing much, perhaps, to extravagant notions of freedom and independence. I fear, too, that in the Presbyterian church, whose principles and policy strongly urge the duty of parental government, it is more neglected than it is among Moravians and Quakers.

Napoleon said, "France wants mothers" And I would say, *"America wants mothers;"* but not such as the great man of blood had in view. She needs not vain parents, to instill into their children a martial spirit, or a love of worldly glory; but such as will teach them that "righteousness which exalteth a nation." If all the children that are now in Christian families were trained thus, they would come into active life just in time to save their imperilled country.

But much more does the church need such parents. The signs of the times are ominous of evil; and there is the more need that "the hearts of our parents be turned to their children, lest the Lord come and smite us with a curse." The piety of the times is too shallow, periodical, and fitful. It is found, by observation, that those converts who have been brought up in pious families, are most devout and uniform.[7] We need, then, more of "the nurture and admonition of the Lord" in the nursery, that we may have more deep-toned and consistent piety in "the household of faith." In many places, the church is declining in numbers, as well as in piety. But if all the children of professors were rightly trained, how many of them would soon be converted, and join the visible church. Nor would the rest drink in, as too many now do, the infidelity of the day.

Loud complaints are heard from every part of the land, that "the laborers are few;" and hence the many calls for "prayer to the Lord of the harvest," that he would "send forth laborers into his harvest." Hence, too, the calls upon our Elkanahs and Hannahs, to bring their young Samuels into the house of the Lord. And as so great a share of ministers have come, hitherto, from pious families, what an increase of such laborers might soon be expected, if all the fathers and mothers in Israel were faithful in training their sons for the service of the Lord. How important, then, in view of all the foregoing considerations, that parents of the present age should follow the example of Abraham, in "commanding their children after them to keep the way of the Lord."

Judges xiii. 12.

"How shall we order the child?"

Lecture 2

Momentous Events

The birth of a child is generally regarded as a trivial event. Even its parents do not estimate it as highly as they ought. Those who are following their son to the gallows, were probably much interested in his birth. But, alas! how much deeper had been their interest, if they had suspected how he was to pain their hearts by his life, and break them by his death. The parents of Gen. Washington rejoiced greatly, no doubt, when their little George was born. But, oh! how much greater would have been their joy, if they had foreseen his glorious career; especially, had they known what inestimable blessings were to come through his hands to the many millions of their fellow men.

And yet there is, belonging to every infant, a far greater importance than we are wont to attach to the most malignant foe, or the best benefactor of our race. It is that which pertains to its immortality. For there is no comparison between time and eternity. At the birth of every child, there is waked into life a soul that will never cease. Its activities and its happiness or woe will continue as long as angels adore and God reigns. This soul is of infinite importance, then, because of its infinite duration.

We are apt to think, too, that the death of a child is a trivial event. Its parents may mourn for it sorely. But it is because of their parental love, and not because of their high valuation of it on the scale of moral beings. During its brief stay on earth, it has written no important history on the mind of any one. And in its early death, its mission to earth seems a failure. But far different is the fact. The close of its life on earth is not the termination of its existence. No; its existence is eternal. And the presumption is, that it will expand and increase in energy forever. Nor is it probable that it will be less active, useful, or happy, than if it had long remained on earth, since all who die in infancy are evidently saved. It is only removed to another sphere of enjoyment and usefulness; and, for aught we know, it is removed thus early, that it may be the earlier and the better prepared for the enjoyment and service assigned it. The death of a child on the very day of its birth, may be as great an event, then, as that of Dr. Chalmers or Daniel Webster; and some of those infants who died by the edict of Herod, may be now before the throne of God, shining in acquirements as vast, and accomplishments as illustrious, as those of Luther or Calvin, Whitfield or Wesley.

Those who have lost young children should be consoled by the thought, then, that their departed ones have left a world of sin and sorrow for one of holiness and bliss; and that while their nurses here were erring and imperfect, their present ones, who "do always behold the face of their Father in heaven," will give them, as "the heirs of salvation," all the care they need. They should say to themselves,

> "They are not dead, these babes of our affection,
>   But gone unto that school,
> Where they no longer need our poor protection,
>   And Christ himself doth rule."

The thought that their children, if still on earth, would be exposed to trouble and sorrow here, and to everlasting woe hereafter, but that now they are in a world where is "fullness of joy and pleasures forevermore"—this thought, I say, should turn their grief to joy, and their mourning to lofty praise.

To their departed children, parents owe no duties; for their destinies are fixed, and nothing that others can do, will relieve or improve them. But many and momentous are the duties which they owe to those still alive. Yet many grieve so excessively over their deceased, as to neglect their living ones. They should rather reflect, that while the former need none, the latter need the utmost of their anxiety and care; that these living ones are exposed to sin, to suffering, and to eternal woe; and that a vast amount of watchfulness and effort is needed to keep them from these evils. And since the Lord, instead of taking these, also, to himself, is still lending them, at such a fearful hazard to their parents, what a solemn responsibility does he thus impose upon them. What a solemn truth, that he spares our children to us at the peril of their souls, and thus makes us responsible for their perdition, if they are lost through our neglect. In the language of the prophet, he "sets us as watchmen over them;" therefore, "if they die in their iniquity, their blood will be required at our hand."

But the grief of some bereaved parents is leading them to neglect their surviving children, not through indifference to them, but through excessive tenderness. The loss of their other children, leads them to idolize their surviving ones. And through excessive and false affection for them, they fail to restrain and guide them as they ought; and thus they ruin them, both for the present and the future world. What folly and sin to fit our living children for hell, because God has taken our others to heaven!

Such, then, is our responsibility in respect to the training of our children, that we should inquire, as Manoah did respecting his son Samson, "How shall we order the child?"

The only means which many employ for the salvation of their children, is that of submitting them to the ceremony of baptism; and even this they often defer till their children are sick unto death. And then, they seem to think there is some charm, magic, or other mysterious influence in the mere ceremony—as if the grace of God were a fluid flowing in the water upon the faces, and then into the souls of their children, fitting them for death and heaven; or as if God had promised to save them on condition that water were applied to them in the name of the Trinity; whereas, no such power or promise is connected with the external ceremony.

Baptism is the answer of a good conscience toward God. (1. Peter,

iii. 21.) And infant baptism is at first the answer, only, of the parent's conscience; for it is then his act, and not that of his child. And it can be his "answer of a *good conscience* toward God," only when he has a proper regard to the *meaning* and *pledge* which the rite implies. Its meaning is, that the child needs "the washing of regeneration." Its pledge is, that the parents will seek the salvation of their child by proper parental nurture. Thus, baptism *operates* nothing, yet *implies* much.

If any should ask, What is the use of infant baptism? I would answer: It is to excite the church, and especially the parents, to more prayer and earnestness in "training up their children in the way they should go." Nor should its influence in this respect be small. As we consider our church relation to our baptized children, how solemnly we have vowed to seek their salvation, and what encouraging promises of success are given us, it should excite us to great earnestness and diligence in "bringing them up in the nurture and admonition of the Lord." And yet, like all other institutions of the gospel, it fails to accomplish all it ought.

I propose to consider, in this and the following discourses, the most important means of moral parental training. They are:

   1. Influence
   2. Authority
   3. Instruction

The first of these will now be considered. By Influence, in distinction from Authority and Instruction, I mean, that secret power by which expression or example impresses the minds of others. Some choose to call it *the power of impression.* It is a kind of mental and moral electricity, by which mankind affect one another. I have placed it first, because it is the first thing that reaches the infant's mind, and the one which impresses it most in its earliest stages, though it is potent in all after life. It will be found, as we have already remarked, that the first year of a child's life is a most important time for molding the head and heart aright, and for giving them the proper direction for life.

The child receives its first ideas through its five senses, Seeing, Hearing, Feeling, Tasting, and Smelling. An impression on any one of these senses, awakens a thought in the mind. For without thought there is no conscious sensation. And, therefore, as I understand it, the way in which chloroform prevents pain in a surgical operation, is by mysteriously interrupting the connection between the senses and the soul. Now, every thought will have an impression on the soul, as the stamp does on wax; and this impression must correspond with the thought that enstamps it. As, then, the soul in childhood is most pliant, and, at the same time, most retentive, it is exceedingly important that the first thoughts which visit it, should be such as will make the best impressions. For the first movements of the mind are like the first shootings of a plant; they determine the direction of its future growth. The first direction taken by a vine, will, probably, decide whether it shall creep along the ground, and be trampled to death under the feet of wild beasts, or whether it shall ascend the oak, and bear its clusters for many generations. It is important, then, that the first objects that fix the gaze of infancy, should be pleasant and winning, not ugly and repulsive. The parents, nurses, and others who approach it, should wear a smiling aspect, not a sad or sour, angry or scowling one.

"I may be thought fanciful," says Babington, "but I certainly think it would be important to keep sour and ill-humored faces out of the nursery, even though such faces were not commonly accompanied by corresponding conduct. I am persuaded, that I have seen a very bad effect produced by a face of this kind, on the countenance of an infant. Is it not reasonable to suppose, that if the infant sympathizes with a smile, it may also sympathize with a scowl, and catch somewhat of the disposition which distorts the features of the nurse." *(Christian Education, p. 37.)*

Nor will counterfeit appearances avail. The child reads the countenance with more readiness and accuracy, and understands the language of the passions more readily, than adults do. Little is many a mother aware how early it detects her false looks, and how much she is doing, at a very early age, to teach her child, by example, to become a deceiver. If she would make the *right* impression, she must use no deception, but *have the right 'feelings',* and leave them to act themselves out, spontaneously.

And so, also, it is important that the first *sounds* which salute the infant ear should be soft and soothing, not boisterous, harsh or frightful. Some people have, by nature or habit, a loud, rough way of speaking and acting. From these the young child should be guarded, as, also, from all harsh and unpleasant sounds. And the same is true as to all its other senses; for impressions on any of them will contribute more or less to determine its disposition — whether it shall be mild and quiet, or whether it shall be wild or willful, morose or turbulent.

And, besides these senses of the body, there are two properties which I shall call *the senses of the soul.* They are Sympathy and Imitativeness. They are evidently twin affections, although sympathy manifests itself slightly at the age of two weeks, and fully at the age of two months; while the other is not called out till four months afterwards. Sympathy is thought by many to be a human weakness. But it is that, in fact, which Divine Wisdom has interwoven in our constitution for wise and noble purposes. True, it can be, and often has been, grievously abused; but its right use is essential to the highest human welfare.

Sympathy is a disposition to feel as others feel. Imitativeness is a disposition to act as others act. And these instincts lie at the foundation of our social natures. Without *sympathy,* we should have no disposition to associate together; and without *imitativeness,* we should not have that likeness of conduct and manners, nor feel that union of interests, which is needful to bind society together. Nor should we acquire what is so essential to our intercourse, a *common language.*

Just so soon as the child begins to feel and act like those around it, it is important that all in its presence should feel and act aright, and thus furnish it with none but proper objects of imitation. For, as before remarked, the infant is an early and accurate observer of the feelings and conduct of others. Whether this fact is owing to its having, in infancy, an instinctive, intuitive knowledge of the language of the passions, a knowledge which it loses when reason comes to supply its place, or whether, like the deaf or the blind, it is more dependent than afterward on its observations, and is the more attentive to looks, and tones, and actions, I will not say. But such is the fact, account for it as we may. And those parents err egregiously, therefore, who talk and act improperly before their child, thinking it will take no notice of them. It is owing, principally, I think, to *sympathy* and *imitativeness,* that the child partakes so much of the disposition and character of its parents. It is often said to "drink them in with the mother's milk." Yes; with her milk, but not in it, nor by it. More properly, it takes them in at its ears and eyes, from its parent's words and actions.

If, during the first year of its life, its parents would be as attentive to the *soul* of their child as they are to its far less important part, the *body,* how much good they might accomplish. Oh, if they would treat it neither as an idol nor as a plaything, but regard it as "a candidate for a glorious immortality," and would practically consider how much it depends on their treatment, whether it eventually prove to be "an embryo angel or an infant fiend," how much anguish they would save both themselves and their child.

Consider, then, dear parents, how important that you cultivate, thus early, these seven senses of your child. Consider that now the plate and camera-obscura of the moral daguerreian is so adjusted as to exclude nearly all other influences, except what emanate from yourselves; and that now you have your best opportunity for

transferring your own moral image—not to a plate of metallic com-
position, but to one of far higher value, the "fleshly table of the heart"
of your own dear child. And remember, that to enstamp the right
image, you must have yourself the right moral character. You must
be Christians, indeed; Christians at home; Christians wearing more
of the lovely, if not less of the sterner aspects of religion, than many
professing parents are wont to exhibit. But this requisite may be your
chief objection to the means of Christian nurture which is now
recommended; and yet it would be peculiarly beneficial to yourselves. For the more lovely and consistent your piety at home, the
better it will be both for yourselves and your offspring. And if you are
faithful with your child at first, you will probably fix on it impressions
that will, in a great measure, determine its career of piety on earth
and blessedness in heaven. To say the least, you will thereby do
much toward giving it an obedient and teachable disposition.

A child that is not yet brought into complete submission, is like
a broken bone, or a limb out of joint; and the sooner it is "reduced,"
the better. For the longer it remains out of place, the more it gets
inflamed or indurated; and, therefore, the more difficult its reduction
becomes. And as in surgery it is necessary to make applications in
order to keep down the inflammation, or to allay it if it be already excited, so, in this case, the right training of the seven senses will prepare the child for the more easy and entire subjection of its will to
the will of its parents.

And there is another means highly recommended, as fitted to
render this subjugation still more easy and complete. I have not
tested it by experience, but it seems philosophical; and I now wonder
that I did not test it when I read of it, many years ago, in the writings
of that able statesman and divine, Dr. Witherspoon. But my attention
has been recalled to it, of late, by reading Rev. Professor Lindley's
"Infant Philosophy."

Dr. Witherspoon thought the experiment should be commenced
when the child is eight months old; Prof. Lindley, when it is only five

or six months old. And the latter advises that the previous months should be improved in securing the child's entire confidence. He particularly cautions parents not to forfeit its confidence by disappointing, tantalising, or trifling with it; among other ways, by "half letting it fall and then catching it again." He urges them, on the contrary, to show themselves, up to the time of commencing this experiment, to be always ready to meet the wants and wishes of the child. I will now give you the outlines of this mode of treatment, mostly in the words of Professor Lindley.

"Call the attention of your child, and give it a toy, or something else that will please it. It is made the more glad by the favor, as connected with your good will, than if received by accident. Yet, to make its pleasure complete, you should sympathize awhile with it in its gratification. But be careful, as soon as it begins to lose its interest in the toy, to take it away, without expressing any regret at its loss; and if it is not more than five or six months old it will not cry after it. But if you ever surrender it after having expressed your will to remove it, you will train it to know that it can overcome you, if it cry sufficiently loud, and storm with sufficient vengeance. In the space of an hour, or after the regret at its loss has died away, you may restore the toy, to be kept as long as the child pleases.

"The next day, select something else, your watch, for instance. Lay it in your child's lap, and assist its delight in its beauty and tick. And again, as its interest begins to flag, put up your watch, and leave your child to its regrets, to its conscious inability to retain its objects of pleasure, and its sense of dependence on your favor.

"The next day, or several days afterward, take another object, a looking-glass, for instance; put it in its lap, guarding it, and congratulating your child as before. And again, at the proper time, remove it, till you restore it the next day; and never give it some things else, simply because it cannot injure them. For, by doing so, you would teach your child that you were bound to reward its privations. This would make it arrogant, and prostrate your authority.

"Continue this process for five or six months, if needful, by means of toys and other things with which your child is pleased." *(Infant Philosophy, pp. 180-4.[8])*

Of this plan Dr. Witherspoon says: "I can assure you, from experience, having literally practiced the method myself, that I never had a child of twelve months old, but would suffer me to take anything from him or her, without the least mark of anger or dissatisfaction. You will easily see how this is to be extended from one thing to another, from contradicting to commanding." (*Witherspoon's Works, vol. 4, p. 136.)*

And Prof. Lindley says: "I know, from experiments which I have made, or have seen made, to the amount of hundreds of cases, the system will, if carefully pursued, bring the child at ten months old into a happy subjection to its parent's will, so that it will cheerfully and without a murmur, surrender to the wish of a parent whatever might be most dear to it." *(Infant Philosophy, pp. 56-7.)*

Again, he says, this system "will secure the complete submission of the child to the will of the parent, without the use of the rod or the asperities of the voice. And all this shall be effected before the child knows the names of his toys. And the infant trained in accordance with this plan until it is twelve months old, will feel no passion of resentment, and will not cry when you take from it any article of which it is most fond, and which you would think at the time absorbed its whole soul. Having never for the first time prevailed over your will, when fairly known, your child has set it down among things which are impossible . . . Neither does any person, infant, child, or man, put forth an act of will . . . for the purpose of obtaining an object which he verily believes to be unattainable. And if you are firm and immovable in what you do and say, the child takes it for granted that your will is, and must necessarily be, the rule of his conduct.

"Two things are now gained to the child. The first is, the perfect peace and quietude of its own mind, while moving within the sphere of your will. The second is, the docility with which it will be ready to receive from you any instructions which it is capable of receiving, and you at the time are ready to give." (pp. 184-5.)

Dr. Dick, "On the Mental Illumination and Moral Improvement of Man," has also recommended this plan. (pp 86-7.) And if it be as efficient as these authors represent, it is an invention of more importance than the steam engine or the magnetic telegraph; for, if it were faithfully tried by all parents, it would work out more important results than could be wrought by lightning or by steam. For what is the increase of velocity or power in the commercial or mechanical world, compared with that cheerful and complete obedience to parental authority which makes men happy and useful in this life, and blessed forever in the life to come?

To say the least of it, a plan so apparently rational, and so highly recommended by the many intelligent ones who have practiced it, is certainly deserving of a faithful trial, especially as the trial would be so safe and easy. Let no parents act as foolishly as I have done. Let them not inconsiderately disregard and neglect it, when its merits can be so safely and so easily tested. "Prove all things: hold fast that which is good." But let the trial be exact and thorough, lest the vast advantages that might otherwise result from this plan should be lost by the defective manner in which it is tested.

Prov. xxii. 15.

"Foolishness is bound in the heart of a child; but the rod of correction will drive it far from him."

Lecture 3

Parental Government an Important Duty

Our text is a declaration, in strong language, that though the disposition and habit of sin is deeply seated in the soul of a child, yet proper parental chastisement will eventually dislodge it. Many in modern times are insisting that the use of the rod, for the purpose of parental correction, is a stupid and barbarous practice. They insist that *moral suasion,* or, at most, that *shame, confinement,* and *privation* are all the means that should be employed to enforce obedience. But their error must be evident; for, as we shall see hereafter, the child's submission, to be both easy and entire, must be effected before it can know enough of the fitness of things to be either reasoned or shamed into obedience, or can be effectually urged to it by imprisonment or privation. And the use of the *rod* — in other words, the infliction of some bodily pain — is the means which God has most plainly appointed for the child's correction. It is mentioned twelve times in his word, as an instrument of authority;[9] and five of them are in relation to children. Besides, *chastisement, scourging* and *stripes,* in evident connection with the use of the rod, are used as many times more.[10] It may be said, that in some of these passages the word *rod* is used figuratively. But what of that, since it is not so used in all of them, and since it would not be proper to use it thus even metaphorically, if it were as improper an instrument of discipline as many would maintain? Since, then, the rod is so plainly the means appointed of God to enforce parental obedience, to discard it utterly is most unwise, if not absolutely impious.

But it is used by many more frequently and more severely than it ought to be; and it is probable that this excessive use of it is what has turned many against it. Nor would it now be needed so much, if the previous treatment of the child had been proper. I verily believe, that if the measures recommended in my last discourse were thoroughly attended to, the rod would rarely be needed. And, some children are of a softer, quieter mold than others. Such may, therefore, be sub-dued without a stroke of the switch or, the hand, even though they have not had the training just alluded to. I have sometimes suc-ceeded, myself, both in the school and the family, without any such chastisements. All I would insist upon is, that *early* and *entire* obedi-ence should be enforced somehow, and certainly by the rod if not otherwise.

Said the Rev. Dr. Hyde to his son, "I have never kept a rod in my house, but I would have my children obey me. I presume you have no recollection of my ever correcting you: but you were taught to mind early, before you had numbered two years." I would that all parents did so. But I fear that many who condemn the use of the rod, fail thereby to enforce obedience by any means; while, on the other hand, I believe that half the stripes which others give are worse than in vain. Punishment is like medicine. Some suffer for the want of it, while others stiffer by taking it too often, and in too great quantities. And many condemn the use of the rod, because they do not distin-guish between the abuse and the right use of it. Their argument is, The rod is used too much; therefore it should not be used at all.

It is proposed to show in this discourse, *that parents are under imperious and solemn obligation to secure the complete obedience of their children.*

In the first place, the duty is repeatedly and earnestly commanded of God, in the following passages of his word: "Chasten thy son while there is hope of him; and let not thy soul spare for his crying." (Prov. xix. 18.) Here is a command to punish a child early and thoroughly —*early*, before he is hopelessly hardened in willfulness; *thoroughly*, that is, as long as is needful to subdue and reform him, however much he may strive by his outcries to induce us to desist.

"Train up a child in the way he should go, and when he is old he will not depart from it." (Prov. xxii. 6.) To "train him in the way he should go," is to "command" him, as Abraham did, and so to enforce the command, that he "shall keep the way of the Lord, to do justice and judgment." (Gen. xvii. 19.) Here, then, we have another commandment to secure the complete obedience of our children.

"Withhold not correction from a child; for, if thou beatest him with the rod, he shall not die. Thou shalt beat him with the rod, and shalt deliver his soul from hell." (Prov. xxiii. 13, 14.) Here we are most directly required to enforce obedience upon our children, as a means of promoting their eternal welfare.

And again: "Correct thy son, and he shall give thee rest; yea, he shall give delight to thy soul." (Prov. xxix. 17.) That *correction* which will cause a child to give "rest" and "delight" to its pious parents, must be reformatory,—such as one, that is, as is said, in our text, to drive sin far from him — such a one as is effected by the rod; and such a one as is said in the foregoing passage to "save his soul from hell". This, then, is a virtual command to secure the complete obedience of our children.

And the same is enjoined by the apostle. "Ye fathers, provoke not your children to wrath; but bring them up the nurture and admonition of the Lord." (Eph. vi. 4.) Now, "the nurture and admonition of the Lord," is such a discipline and instruction as God bestows upon his people. And he "chasteneth and scourgeth every son whom he receiveth." (Heb. xii. 6.) Here, again, we are required, then, to secure the complete obedience of our children.

Thus positively and repeatedly has God commanded this duty; nor can parents have any more liberty to neglect this, than any other duty which he has enjoined. And yet, how many who profess to take the word of God for their guide, are just as negligent of family government, as if he had never commanded it! Oh, to what a fearful reckoning will such be called, on the great day of final accounts!

But, in the second place, the *importance of filial obedience* will show more strikingly the duty of enforcing it. As God has made us social beings, authority on the one hand, and submission on the other, are absolutely necessary to the welfare of the family, the church, and the state. Every community needs, then, its laws, and it appropriate persons to administer them; and so far as disobedience prevails, it is ruinous to the welfare of community. It is as much, therefore, the duty of the ruler *to enforce* as of the subject to *yield* obedience. It is important, all will say, that children should "obey their parents in the Lord." All must see it needful to the welfare of society, and especially to the children themselves, that they be completely and constantly obedient; and a disobedient child is always looked upon as a very bad one. But, wherein is it worse for him to disobey, than for his parents to let him do it? He probably knows but little of the evil consequences of a disobedient course; while his parents know, or ought to know, that by allowing him to disobey habitually, they are training him to be a trouble in the family, a pest in society, and a victim of unhappiness in time, and of misery in eternity.

On this point, Babington says: "Without filial obedience, everything must go wrong . . . Is not a disobedient child guilty of a manifest and habitual breach of the fifth commandment? And is not a parent who suffers this disobedience to continue, when he knows he is armed with sufficient power to overcome it, an habitual partaker of its offense against that commandment? How can those who are thus criminal, hope for God's blessing on any part of their conduct? . . . In proportion as filial obedience is calculated to smooth the way for true religion, filial disobedience must produce the opposite effect. The parent who habitually gives way to it, has appalling reason to apprehend that he is educating his child, not for heaven, but for hell." *(Practical View, pp.* 99–101.)

It was evidently this view of the importance of obedience, which led Solomon to say, (Prov. xiii. 24,) "He that spareth his rod hateth his child; but he that loveth him, chasteneth him betimes." To those who are kept by a false, morbid tenderness from chastising their children when they need it, and whose "tender mercies are therefore cruel," this declaration of the wise man may seem preposterous. But it is evidently the sober truth of God. For, surely, we show most genuine love to our children, when we seek their highest welfare; and this we do, in thoroughly chastening them for their good. Again: It is equally evident, that the greatest cruelty to our children consists in doing them the greatest injury; and this is done, if we spare the rod when needed. Said Abbot, "If there is any cruelty that is truly frightful, it is the cruelty of a falsely indulgent parent." *(Mother at Home, p. 70.)*

Again: We manifest most love for our children when we practice most self-denial for their good. And this we do, when we judiciously chastise them for the purpose of correcting their faults, or to render them obedient — doing it when it is very painful to ourselves, but needful to them; while those who spare the rod, in such circumstances, do it not merely out of sympathy for their children, but out of regard to themselves. They spare the rod for the sake of sparing themselves the pain of inflicting it. It is, therefore, a cruel selfishness which leads them to neglect it, or, in the language of Solomon, to "hate" their children. And how much better is this selfishness, which ruins its object, than that of the debauches?

The rod is needful to the child, because, as the text tells us, it will drive far from him that "foolishness" or sin, which is bound up in him; and because, as the same wise man elsewhere says, it will "deliver his soul from hell." His habitual insubordination to the will of his father on earth, will make him the more stubborn toward his Father in heaven; and thus may eventually prevent his submission and salvation. How cruel, then, to withhold the rod that would drive far from him a rebellion so ruinous.[11] And if, as the apostle affirms, he who hates a brother is a murderer, then, by unavoidable inference, he who hates his child (by sparing the rod) is a murderer. He inflicts death, not on the body, but on the soul. He murders the soul of his child, as I should the body of mine, if I saw him starving, and withheld the food that would save him from death; or, (to make the parallel most complete,) if I saw him drowned, and would not try to restore him, lest my tender heart should suffer on seeing the pains that would attend his restoration from suspended animation.

I know this sin lacks one dark feature of atrocity—that of *malignant intention.* The parent who ruins his child by indulgence, does not wish to injure him. But, though this relieves, it does not remove, his guilt. The command, "Thou shalt not kill," virtually enjoins all needful care and effort to preserve the lives of others. The parent, then, who ruins his child through indulgence, carelessness, or selfish disregard of his highest welfare, is guilty, in the eye of heaven, of soul-murder.

I am well aware that this charge may seem severe. But all its severity lies in its truth. I would speak with all tenderness; but I must say, in sincerity, that the man who brings up his son in disobedience, thus training him to be not only a turbulent and vicious member of society, but a tenant of the pit of woe, is committing a worse sin than theft or robbery. Taking a thousand dollars from a neighbor's desk, or plundering his granary or store—what is that to the ruin of a soul, and that the soul of his own son, whom he has been the means of bringing into life, as well as of sending to eternal death?

If I had a son under the care of others, I would rather have them rob him of all his property, mutilate his limbs, and inflict all but death upon him, than bring him up as many are brought up — in ruinous indulgence and utter disobedience. For what would it profit him to have the whole world, its possessions and pleasures, if he should lose his own soul? Ah! it will be found, in the judgment, that some of the worst of crimes have been committed by parents upon their children, by withholding the rod. And what anguish must such parents feel, when they find that, by failing to "beat their children with a rod," they have failed to "deliver their souls from hell."

Said Dr. Witherspoon, in writing to his friend, on the *government* of children, "There is no part of your duty, as a Christian or a citizen, which will be a greater service to the public or comfort to yourself." What shall we think, then, of those professing Christians who are as neglectful of this duty as if they cared not for the commands of God, or for the welfare of their children, or of others? For one, I know of nothing in which they need more to be reformed, and nothing in which their complete reformation would be more beneficial to themselves and their children, the church and the world.

And there is another account on which it is important that Christian parents should be faithful in the government of their children. It is, that they may deliver the church from a certain slander under which it is suffering. It is, that "the children of Christians, and especially of ministers, elders, and deacons, are more disobedient than those of impenitent parents." I call it a slander, for it is not true that the children of professors, in general, are more ungoverned than those of non-professors. Examination has proved the contrary. Still there are too many facts which favor this slander. For it is, indeed, true, that many Christians,—yes, many ministers—are lamentably deficient in family government. And when a child disobeys, we spontaneously blame both the child for disobeying, and the parent for *letting him* disobey. Especially do we blame the Christian who suffers it. Every professor, then, who fails to govern his household, helps to spread and confirm this slander. On this account, therefore, it is the more important that he reform. If all the children of the church were as well governed as many of them are, religion would be far more respected and prospered.

Especially is it important that ministers, officers, and conspicuous members of the church, should govern their households well, their examples being so influential. This was, doubtless, the reason why those deficient in this duty were not to be admitted to the offices of bishops and deacons in the church. "A bishop," said Paul, "must be blameless—one that ruleth well his own house, having his children in subjection." And, "Let the deacons be the husband of one wife, ruling their children and their houses well." (I Tim. iii. 2, 4, 12.) This, too, is probably the reason why Eli was so signally punished when "his sons made themselves vile, and he restrained them not."[12] It was to counteract his evil example.

Many will insist that they cannot govern their children. But this excuse must involve either great weakness or great wickedness. All parents possessing common sense, are, or ought to be, able to make a young child obey; and if it be but once thoroughly subdued by the time it is a year old, it will always be easy to govern it. If any are so weak that they cannot make such a child obey, they are not fit to have the care of children. The good of the children themselves, and of society, requires that they be taken from such parents, and put under competent guardians. And if any fathers and mothers that plead inability, would scorn this imputation of weakness, let them *assert* and *put forth* their ability. But if they are actually able to do this momentous ditty of governing their children, how wicked in them to plead inability.

Some insist, that the art of family government is a natural gift, a kind of instinctive skill, which none but certain of nature's favorites can possess. But few notions are more absurd. Parents never fail in government through the unavoidable deficiency of tact, but because they voluntarily fail to seek and employ it. Whatever of knowledge, judgment, or skill is employed by those who "rule their own houses well," is possessed by many, and might be possessed by all who govern ill, or rather govern not at all.

Some probably succeed well, because they happened to fall on the right methods of securing obedience, and get confirmed in them by custom, or because they follow the correct methods of their parents; while others have failed, because they were not led aright by providence or parental example. But they need not have failed. Nor would they have failed, if they had sought that instruction on the subject which they needed, and had put it properly in practice.

It is truly astonishing how little the most of parents inquire, or even think, about the proper modes and means of enforcing obedience. Some have books on the subject, yet almost never consult them. And rarely do they inquire in any way, "How shall we order the child?" but act wholly on occasion or impulse. Nor is it any wonder at all that such heedless ones should fail. They must fail in every other difficult thing to which they give as little attention. It is truly amazing how little principle and firmness many otherwise judicious people bring to the momentous concern of parental government. They are so destitute of purpose and plan, so impulsive and fickle, no wonder they are so unsuccessful. They must fail in every critical and arduous undertaking which they manage with such a slack and careless hand.

But it is not thus that they attend to their other affairs. Many who value themselves much on being skillful and business-like, thorough and energetic, in all their other concerns, are utterly unskillful and bungling, loose and negligent,—in the far more important business of governing their children. Why! if a man who has now no control over his children, would apply himself to the task of subduing them, with as much resolution and care, energy and perseverance, as he puts forth *in the breaking of a colt,* he would no more fail in the one than in the other. And how much more important to train a child for usefulness on earth and blessedness in heaven, than the breaking of a horse to the saddle or the draft.

The truth, then, is, that all parents who have common sense can govern their children, if they will but duly inquire after the right way of doing it, and will pursue it with proper caution and firmness. And those who neglect to do so, are showing no little contempt to the command of God, and are doing incalculable injury to their children, to their country, and to the church of Christ. Nor will the Lord accept their plea of inability, but frown the more upon them for making it.

I have treated this point the more at length, and earnestly, because I verily believe that most of parents are sadly neglectful in regard to it; and because I am very anxious to persuade such to resolve fully and firmly, that from henceforth they will "do with their might" this all-important duty. I am the more anxious to have them accept this resolution, as it would prompt them to study this duty as they have never done before; and thus they would be the better prepared to follow me in our next inquiry, viz *How are parents to secure the early and complete obedience of their children?* which inquiry will be the theme of the next two discourses.

Another advantage of such a resolution, would be, the discovery that the proverb, "Where there is a will there is a way," is most emphatically true in regard to this duty. Half the difficulties thought to be in the way of governing children, are conjured up by lazy indecision. When parents firmly resolve to do this duty, a holy courage will follow, and many a fancied difficulty will be put to flight. Let the resolution, then, be forthwith adopted.

Prov. xxiii. 24.

"The father of the righteous shall greatly rejoice: and he that begetteth a wise child shall have joy of him."

Lecture 4

Government by Authority

*I*n a previous discourse we considered, in connection with these words, the sacred obligation of parents to secure and maintain the complete obedience of their children. This obedience includes no less than the entire subjugation of the will of the child to the will of his parents. And we come now to consider the way in which this subjugation should be effected. To the proper exercise of parental authority, four things are requisite. One is, that the child be required to obey, simply *on the ground of the parent's right to command.* Another is, that *obedience be enforced while the child is very young.* A third is, that this obedience be *complete, prompt,* and *uniform.* And the other is, that when punishment is necessary to enforce obedience, *it should be administered with much judgment and discretion.* We shall need to dwell on each of these at considerable length, apart.

1. This obedience should be required, we have said, simply *on the ground of the parent's right to command.* Young children stand in the like relation of authority to the "fathers of their flesh," that we all do to "the Father of spirits." God himself has instituted this relation, in the command, "Honor thy father and mother;"[13] for he so recognizes and illustrates it, in the following declaration and inquiry: "A son honoreth his father—if I then be a Father, where is mine honor?"[14] Parental authority, then, is a parental *theocracy.* Fathers and mothers are God's vicegerents in the family. And to "bring up their children in the *nurture and admonition of the Lord,*" when they require obedience of them, it should be on the same ground that God claims it of us all; that is, on the ground of *right to command.* There are other

reasons, it is true, why we should obey him; and he sometimes urges them. But many of his commands are such that no other reason can be given for obeying them, but mere divine authority. And that should always be reason enough. It was concerning such authority that David said, "I opened not my mouth, because thou didst it;"[15] that Christ said, "Even so, Father, for so it seemed good in thy sight;"[16] and that Paul said, "Nay but O man, who art thou that repliest against God."[17] And so it is in regard to the command of a parent to his young children. They cannot, need not, know the why and the wherefore of it. Enough that parents have a right to utter and enforce such a command; whereas, if they have no right to enforce it, without showing the reason of it, (as the advocates of the suasion system contend,) the complete obedience of the child could not be secured. For, as it will be shown hereafter, if the child obeys not till he is old enough to see the reasonableness of obeying, he would never become habitually obedient; and when he did comply, he could not be said to submit to his parents' authority, so much as to their reasoning.

As early as he can understand it, the child should be told that he is compelled to obey, not to gratify the will of his parents, but for his own good, and the good of others. And this important truth should always be kept before his mind. It is true, too, that as his mind matures, he should be shown more and more how reasonable and important are the commands imposed upon him; but not as a means of enforcing obedience. The authority of the parents should always be held out as the all-sufficient reason for obeying their commands. But he should be shown it as an after-work, in teaching him to *govern himself.* And if they have previously, by dint of authority, secured a full control over his will, it will be all the easier to teach him self-government.

As the "check" or "gag-rein" assists the coachman to manage his horses, so the complete and habitual submission of the child to his parents will make it the easier for them to guide him by the rein of reason. A submissive spirit is a docile one, while a stubborn one is blind and reckless.

2. *Obedience ought to be enforced while the child is quite young.* Just so soon as, by language or looks, tones or gestures, he can learn the will of his parents, it is time to begin the work of enforcing his obedience; and if the measures recommended in my second discourse have been faithfully tried upon him, I believe the task of securing his obedience will not be very difficult. But whether they have or have not been attended to, the work should generally be begun before he is a year old. Often it is happily begun at the age of nine months. It should commence thus early for two reasons. One is, that then the will is most pliant and easily subdued; and the other is, that then the *habit* of obedience can be most easily and permanently established.

But many parents, instead of subduing the will of the child thus early, are doing much to render it more stubborn. They will not cross his inclinations themselves, nor allow any one else to do it. He is permitted to domineer over the older children and servants, they being required to give up their seats, and everything else that the little capricious tyrant happens to desire. And the reason given for doing so is, "The child is young,"—the very reason why it should not be done. For, the more he is indulged, the more capricious and willful he will become, and, therefore, the more difficult it will be to subdue him afterward. Instead, then, of forming in him this habit of domineering, they should form in him, now, when it can be done most easily, the habit of obedience. Nor is it a matter of small importance that it be done so early that he cannot recollect having ever disobeyed; for the habit thus early formed, will render his obedience most easy and sure.

So, also, in regard to the child's passions. Many parents allow him, (because he is so little,) to be for a long while impatient, petulant, and wrathful, thinking, it would seem, that they must bear with his peevishness and spite as long as they can. But the greater their forbearance, the greater their cruelty. For these adverse feelings are painful; and the longer they allow him to indulge them, the longer they leave him to remain unhappy. How much more happy is the sweetly subdued child than the one who remains rebellious. Furthermore, the longer an evil disposition is indulged, the more confirmed it is; consequently, the more reproof and punishment are needed to subdue it. It may be said of willfulness and anger, as of certain diseases, that the longer they are allowed to run, the more they will "rage." The more, then, they will injure the constitution; consequently, the more painful and difficult the cure. How much kinder, as well as wiser, to "nip these evils in the bud."

"You should establish, as soon as possible," says Dr. Witherspoon, "an entire and absolute authority. It should be early, that it may be absolute; and absolute, that it may not be severe. If parents are too long in beginning to exert their authority, they will find the task very difficult. Children habituated to indulgence for a few of their first years, are exceedingly impatient of restraint, and if they happen to be of stiff and obstinate tempers, can hardly be brought into a quiet and placid submission; whereas, if taken in time, there is hardly any temper but what may be made to yield. And by early habit, the subjection becomes easy to themselves." *(Witherspoon's Works, vol. 5, p. 134.)*

But if we have not begun in time to govern our children, we must be the more resolute, firm, and thorough in our efforts to subdue their wills, as the task will then be more difficult. For to give them up in discouragement to willfulness and disobedience, as many, do, would be most disastrous. The subjugation of their wills is, therefore, so important, that we should by no means fail of effecting it.

The first effort to enforce obedience is by far the most important one. The occasion and circumstances should, therefore, be cautiously selected. The first enforcement of authority should be in some simple and clear case of duty, in which it is perfectly evident that the child understands the command, and disobeys it through anger or willfulness. Indeed, the like caution should be had in all cases of discipline. But in the first case it is most especially important. We should be careful, moreover, never to correct a child when he does not deserve it; for, as Raffles observes, "Where, in one instance, the infliction has been unjust, the justice of it in every other instance will be questioned."

3. The child's obedience should be *complete, prompt* and *uniform.* In no one instance in which he ought to obey, should he be allowed to disobey. Many may think it will cost them too much time and effort to be thus strict in parental discipline. But it is the very best way to save them both time and trouble. If you allow your child, at any time, to disobey, you teach him that he can, and thus encourage him to do so; and thus you prolong your contest for mastery over him. But if you never suffer him, in one instance, to disobey, you will soon convince him that disobedience is impossible; and then he will yield at once to all your commands. For neither child nor adult will ever attempt what he believes to be impossible. Though he ever so much desires and tries to do a thing, yet just so soon as he finds it impossible, he ceases from the attempt, and soon after from the desire, to do it.

This, then, is the first and most important lesson to be taught a child—the utter impossibility of disobeying his parents. Nor will it be difficult, if you begin early, and are careful for awhile never to suffer him to disobey, to teach him the lesson that the thing is impossible.

Professor Lindley illustrates this, by the way in which the farmer manages his colt. For the laws of habit are much alike in man and brute. Human nature can, therefore, be learned and illustrated by the actions of the lower animals. "Let him take his colt," says the Professor, "at one, two, or three days old, each day in succession, and hold it, *without letting it break from him;* and this repeated, three or four times in succession, should he then let it loose for three years, and catch it again, it would scarcely make an effort to escape.

The reason is, the impression of impossibility of escape is grounded in him." *(Infant Philosophy, p. 156.)*

Many may suppose, too, that the enforcement of such complete obedience must be severe. But it is, in fact, the best way to prevent severity; for it prevents a vast amount of scolding and whipping on the part of the parents, and of pain, impatience, and anger on the part of the child. How much better for him to be so trained as to yield an unreluctant obedience, than to be bawled and beaten into it, in opposition to his angry, stubborn will? But on this point let us listen again to Dr. Witherspoon. He says:

"The authority ought, also, to be *absolute,* that it may *not be severe.* The more complete and uniform a parent's authority is, the offenses will be more rare, punishment will be less needed, and the more gentle kind of punishment will be abundantly sufficient. We see, everywhere about us, examples of this. A parent that has obtained, and knows how to preserve, authority, will do more by a look of displeasure, than another by the most passionate words, and even blows. It holds universally in families and schools that those who keep the strictest discipline give the fewest strokes. I have frequently remarked that parents, even of the softest tempers, and who are famed for their indulgence to their children, do, notwithstanding, correct them more frequently, and even more severely, (though to very little purpose,) than those who keep up their authority. The reason is plain. Children, by foolish indulgence, become often so adverse and petulant in their tempers, that they provoke their easy parents past endurance, so that they are obliged, if not to strike, at least to scold them, in a manner as little to their own credit as to the children's profit. There is not a more disgusting sight than the impotent rage of a parent who has no authority." (*Vol. 5, p.* 134.)

But when I say that parents should maintain a complete control over their children, I do not mean that they should notice everything which they deem improper in them. Many minor improprieties they would do well to overlook, lest they should weaken their authority by a habit of incessant fault-finding. What I mean is, that whenever they do require or forbid anything, they should never, in one instance, allow themselves to be disobeyed. It is important that, at first, their commands be few, and relate to things of most consequence. Many err egregiously here. Said Dr. Dick, "No command, either by look, word, or gesture, should be given, which is not intended to be enforced and obeyed. It is the rock on which most split in infantile education, that while they almost always are giving commands to their children, they are not punctually obeyed, and seem to consider the occasional violation of their injunctions a very trivial fault, or as a matter of course. There is no practice more common than this, and none more ruinous to the authority of parents, and to the best interests of their offspring. The rule, therefore, should be absolute, that every command ought to be enforced." *(Dick's Works, vol. 5, p. 88.)*

This language is none too strong, for the conduct which it condemns is almost universal. And many parents utter a hundred unobeyed commands in a single day. No wonder, then, that they have so little parental control. For when their command is first given, the child knows not whether they expect or, even intend to be obeyed. Hence, they have to repeat the command, often many times, and with additional declarations that they are in earnest, yet fail to be believed till they begin to punish.

And this repetition of a command is as unwise as it is unavailing. If a command is powerless, what is the use of repeating it? It is adding nought to nought. Resort should be had to something else. Let your child know that you never *repeat* a command; that when told to do a thing, there must be obedience or punishment; and then the command will need no repetition.

And the child should not only obey *every* command, but obey it *immediately*. All delay of submission is protracted rebellion. Yet many parents seem to think, if they make him submit finally, no matter how long they are in battling him into submission. But all the while that they allow him to delay obedience, they are teaching him disobedience. Until he is made to obey in every case *immediately,* there is a continuance of the war; and each future instance of submission will cost another battle.

The early habit of entire and prompt obedience secures several important advantages. Not only does it save a great deal of time and distress in reproof and punishment, but a great deal of perplexity and trouble when the child is sick. It is often very difficult to make a sick child take his medicine. Abbot tells us of the death of one who refused to take it, and whose mother failed to compel him to take it. But the child who knows not how to disobey, will take it without hesitation. This saves both the parent and the child a vast amount of pain and trouble. Besides, the ungoverned child is apt to be much more impatient and peevish in sickness than others, and thus he injures himself and others, much and needlessly. And it is very difficult, in such cases, to punish or reprove him; whereas, if he had been previously well governed, much, if not all, of this evil might have been prevented. The usually kind, yet firm voice of his parents, would be sufficient to allay his irritations, and keep him quiet.

Again, many children are very troublesome on account of their habits of being noisy, of running away, of getting into mischief, and of meddling with everything within their reach. They have to be watched and called after continually. But this is not the case with those children who are trained to exact and immediate obedience. They will venture on nothing that is forbidden them; or if they do, a word is enough to recall them. Some insist that they cannot keep their children from things forbidden them. But you can teach even your domestic animals this; and can you not teach the child as much? All that is needful is *to begin in time,* and, in every instance, to punish him so severely, that he will be afraid to do the thing again.

Many parents fail in accepting, not only a late, but *a reluctant, partial, half-way* obedience. For instance; they tell the child to leave something with which he is meddling. But he moves not. They then repeat the command more sternly, or threaten him. But still he persists. And after many unavailing threats, they seize and drag the child away from the forbidden object. Now this is substituting for parental authority mere animal force. Instead of making the child do what he is commanded, it is *doing it for him.*

Sometimes they tell the child to leave off beating the pan or the barrel. But he beats on, although he does not strike it so hard as before. They next tell him to leave off entirely. And then he strikes toward it, without intending to hit it, thus manifesting as much disobedience of spirit as ever. This, to say the least, is trifling with parental authority, and should never be allowed. For a child will never become truly obedient till he is made properly to "honor his father and mother." Parents who allow themselves to be put off with anything short of prompt and full obedience, are like the man who shuts his door "to," but does not push it far enough to let the latch fall and fasten it; consequently, it may be pressed open again by every opposing influence.

4. When punishment is needed to enforce authority, it should be employed *with much judgment and discretion.* It is desirable to dispense with the rod whenever obedience can be so cured without the use of it. But if it must be used, it should be plied in such a way as to secure submission by the fewest strokes. Many parents make the more severity needful, by their own indiscretion. Some needlessly exasperate the child, by irritating language or treatment, before they chastise him; and thus it requires more stripes to subdue him. They should manifest no anger at him; but give him, as far as they can, to understand that they punish for his own good and, that of the household; for this will give each stroke a greater subduing power, and render the fewer needful. But others err in an opposite direction. In their unwise tenderness, they give the child a few light blows, just enough to make him more angry and stubborn. And then they stop and ask if he is going to submit. Finding that he is not, they ply the rod a little longer and a little harder than at first, yet only enough to make him still more angry and stubborn; and then they

stop again to ask if he is going to yield. But he storms out his wrath more lustily than ever. And thus onward, the parents increase their severity just enough to make him more and more obstinate, till they are tempted to give up the endeavor to subdue him. And if they should do so, it would so encourage and confirm him in his obstinacy, that there would be little hope of his yielding afterward. They should conquer him then, if they would conquer him at all.[18]

But the proper way is, to be more severe at the commencement. Probably, if they had been doubly severe at the beginning, the child would at once have submitted; and this would have saved him and his parents a vast amount of pain and trouble. They should learn wisdom from Bonaparte, in quelling the mob in Paris. Instead of firing blank cartridges at first, as is often done to frighten the mob, (but which only emboldens them the more, and makes it more difficult to subdue them,) he mowed down many of them at once, with a volley of balls, by which they were at once alarmed and routed. And afterward, he fired his blank cartridges, thus saving a vast amount of bloodshed.

More on the subject of government may be expected in the next discourse.

Eph. vi. 4.

"And ye fathers, provoke not your children to wrath; but bring them up in the nurture and admonition of the Lord."

Lecture 5

Government in Love

*I*n a previous discourse, it was maintained, that children should obey their parents on the same ground that all men should obey God; that in, on the ground of their authority. But there is another element in the government of God. It is *love*. "Whom the Lord loveth he chasteneth, and scourgeth every son whom he receiveth." "As many as I love I rebuke and chasten."[19] So, on the other hand, he requires our obedience to be prompted by love to him. Love is the fountain from which all acceptable obedience must flow. It follows, then, that to "bring up our children," in all respects, "in the nurture and admonition of the Lord," like him we must be prompted by love to chastise them, and secure from them an obedience, filial and affectionate. Properly to "honor his father and mother," the child must both *fear* and *love* them. And as "Love, and love only, is the loan of love," we should always show a warm affection and kindness toward our children. Even when we need to chastise them, we should show that, like our heavenly Father, we "do not afflict willingly," but "for their profit."[20] And having secured their love, we shall find it a powerful aid in securing their obedience. For then they will be as unwilling to grieve us and forfeit our approbation by transgression, as to feel the smartings of the switch. Not only are love and fear compatible, but they enhance each other.

Many maintain opposite errors on this subject. Some insist that the child should be ruled by love alone. But our Father in heaven rules both by love and fear. And so should every father on earth rule. If parents do not need to threaten and punish, why is it done by "the Lord of all?" The truth is, that at the early age at which the habit of

obedience needs to be firmly seated, love cannot operate with
sufficient power to secure submission. Psychology, as well as the
example and command of God, teach that the threatening and
infliction of punishment are then needed. And they are often needed
afterward. For often is love too feeble to secure obedience. Indeed,
nothing is obedience, strictly speaking, but what is done out of defer-
ence to authority.[21] But the remarks of the present discourse are
intended mainly for those who err in the opposite direction, of governing by terror or pain alone.

Many parents, instead of promoting the love and confidence of
their children, are doing much to awaken their hatred and distrust.
They are, therefore, forbidden in the text to do so. "And ye fathers,
provoke not your children to wrath; but bring them up in the nurture
and admonition of the Lord." In these words, two things are spoken
of as in opposition, the one forbidden and the other enjoined. We
are here required not to irritate our children, but, on the contrary,
to train them in that affectionate way of which God is our example.
I shall, therefore, take occasion, from the text, to consider some of
the ways in which parents provoke their children to wrath, and
thereby hinder their right moral training.

Many irritate their children needlessly, by their own evident impatience and passion. Such ill-natured inflictions are injurious in two
respects. The man who beats his child in anger, will be likely to beat
him too severely; for passion indulged in, is seldom safe. He who has
not sufficient self-control to subdue his own temper before he takes
the rod, will rarely restrain himself sufficiently while using it. Every
one who finds, as he is about to punish his child, that there is wrath
in his bosom, would do well to heed the words of Socrates, who said
to his servant, "I would beat you, if I were not angry." The punishment should be postponed till passion subsides.

Yet many say, as one man did to Dr. Witherspoon, "I can never
chastise my child unless I am angry with him." The doctor's reply
was, "Then you should not punish him at all." But a better answer

would have been, "You can punish your child out of the purest love; and you ought always to do so, when the good of your child requires it." The object of discipline should be the child's good, always; the gratification of the parent's passion, never. And they who will punish a child only when they are angry, betray great weakness and want of principle.

But the greater evil resulting from such anger is, that it tends to defeat the proper end of chastisement, which is the moral improvement of the child. Those who are prompted by passion to punish, are apt to overlook the *criminality* of his conduct, and to punish him only on account of the *injury* he has done, and done, perhaps, by accident; and whatever be the fault for which the rod is applied, if he sees that the infliction is prompted by passion, he will regard it, not as "the rod of correction," but of *parental wrath.* And then, no moral benefit can result from it. But how different would be the impression and result, if he saw that while his parents were chastising him they loved him as much as ever, and that every stripe was as painful to their hearts as to his body! This mode would be suited to promote his sorrow, submission, and reformation, while the other would make him more angry and stubborn than before. How unwise, then, are those parents who tell their child they are angry with him for his ill conduct! How much better to tell him they are distressed and grieved!

"Punishments," says Babington, "should be employed reluctantly; and yet how often are they inflicted in such a way that there is no reluctance apparent, but they appear to afford a gratification. It would give me pain to describe the scenes that I have witnessed, when a child has been under the correction of a passionate, ill-humored parent. Certainly, punishment, under such circumstances, takes a most offensive form, and is likely to do much more harm than good." (*Practical View, p.* 114.)

Many provoke their children to wrath, in not chastising them sufficiently to subdue them. They slap or switch them just enough to make them the more angry, and leave them to pout or bawl, which only makes the case worse. A child should never be left, after chastisement, in an angry or sullen mood; never. While he should not be punished for crying from pain, he always should for crying from anger; nor should the chastisement cease till his spirit is subdued.

Many needlessly stir up the anger of their child, by severe looks and language, before or during the infliction of punishment; and many may err, as I have done, in assuming a stern manner for the purpose of awakening the more fear in the child. I am now convinced, that a mild, affectionate, yet serious, determined manner is much the most effective one. It will secure the parent against the suspicion of being angry, and thus give his reproof the more power. In the words of Dr. Dick, again, "Reproof or correction, given in a rage, and with words of fury, is always considered as the effect of weakness and want of self-command, and uniformly frustrates the purpose it was intended to subserve." (Vol. 5, p. 88.)

Many provoke their children by the morose or irritating manner in which they utter their commands. By the severity of their looks and tones, they make the impression that the duty commanded is an odious one; consequently, the child braces himself in wrath, against it. Whereas, if the same duty had been required in a mild and affectionate manner, his first impression would have been that the duty was right and agreeable; consequently, he would have at once obeyed. And some parents command, not only in an irritating way, but in a way indicating that they do not expect to be obeyed, till they have scolded and switched awhile; whereas they should do it in a way indicating that they fully expect immediate obedience.

Many provoke their children by a profusion, not only of bitter reproaches, but of odious epithets. "Meanness," "badness," "villain," "scamp," "dog," and the like, are the offensive terms which they often apply to those who are, or should be, very dear to them. Such language, coarse and cruel, seems intended to irritate; and it certainly has the effect. It may be well, at times, to reason and remonstrate affectionately with our children, in order to show them the evil and folly of their doings. But all angry, boisterous rebukes, and hard names are pernicious. And, generally speaking, if one solemn rebuke is not enough to bring them to obey, it is vain to repeat it. Those, therefore, who scold most, govern least. If, then, we would have obedient children, we should reprove but once before we chastise effectually.

Many provoke their children by their *austerity* and *distance.* We should be so reserved and dignified in our conduct toward them as to avoid "the familiarity which breeds contempt;" yet we should be so affectionate and companionable as to win their love and confidence. By keeping them at a distance, and treating them austerely, we shall provoke their dislike and distrust. The dislike thus awakened, would not be so much a high ebullition of anger, as a settled coldness and hate. This would greatly increase the difficulty of maintaining proper dominion over them. Those who govern thoroughly, yet austerely, do better than those over-fond and weak-minded ones who do not govern at all. It is better still, by far, to do it thoroughly, and, at the same time, with affection and due familiarity.

Another way of provoking to wrath, is by *favoritism.* Many parents feel more attachment to some of their offspring than to others; and manifest it in a way that awakens envy toward their favorites, and resentment against themselves; the anger thus awakened will render it the more difficult to keep in subjection these dissatisfied ones.

And another way in which children are provoked to anger, is by withholding the approbation and praise that is due them when they do well, and by failing to encourage them onward, in the right way. Children are apt, it is true, to desire more praise than is due, and to make a bad use of it. We should, therefore, bestow it discreetly, and be careful to make them understand that they have no claim upon us for doing their duty; that we are not paying for their past, nor purchasing their future obedience, but are showing how much it gratifies us to have them act right. Yet we should watch their evil more than their good conduct, as it is more needful to them. And it is a very mistaken notion that love is necessarily blind to the faults of its object.

> "I say such love is never blind, but rather
>   Alive to every, to the minutest spot
> Which was its object, and which hate supposed
>   So vigilant and searching dreams not of."
> *Browning.*

Still, it is very important that we take favorable notice of the good conduct of our children; for they need such encouragement. I have known some who suffered much for the want of it. They were under strict, severe treatment; and, as they were still dull and heedless, they were supposed to be peculiarly perverse. But it was not so. They had their good qualities, yet nothing to call them out; but were completely disheartened by hearing no kind words — nothing but unceasing censure for stupidity and stubbornness. They needed, now and then, a kind word of praise and persuasion, to inspirit them. In one instance, I knew a change of treatment to take place, and the result was a happy one. "The stupid, stubborn girl" became a respectable woman and wife.

To the Colossians, Paul said, "Fathers, provoke not your children to anger, lest they be discouraged." And it is this incessant fault-finding, and this utter absence of approbation, which are most apt to promote that continual irritation which ends in discouragement. Children, treated in this way, are often heard to say, "It is of no use for us to try to please our parents. For when we do the best we can, we hear nothing but an eternal ding-dong of complaint and blame." And then they give up trying to please. If such parents would test "the omnipotence of kindness," they would find it much to their own comfort, and far more to the welfare of their children.

Finally, parents provoke their children to wrath by *improperly indulging them.* They foster thereby a fastidious, arrogant, irritable disposition. It is mainly by such management that the "spoiled child" is made. Petted ones are usually impatient and passionate ones; and in proportion as their wills and wishes have been previously indulged, will be their restiveness and wrath, when their inclinations happen to be crossed and crossed they often must be when they go abroad. And this will render it the more difficult to govern them.

It is evident from observation, that those children who are properly restrained, are, generally speaking, far more affectionate than those who are excessively indulged. I believe the most grievous cases of filial ingratitude and cruelty have been committed by those who have been most humored.

Thus we see it is important to keep from provoking our children in these various ways, because of its bearing on *parental government*. But it is equally important, on account of its bearing on parental *instruction;* and it is no less by teaching, than by restraining our children, that we are to train them up in the way they should go. The influence of anger on parental instruction is both *direct* and *indirect*.

Its *indirect* influence is through parental authority. For the most obedient children are most attentive to what is taught them. See that mother, who has no control over her child. She is trying to teach him the alphabet. She points to A, and says "What letter is that?" But he pays no attention to her. She reproves him, and pointing again to the letter, she says, what is that? still he pays no attention. She repeats again and again, to no purpose. He is so accustomed to disregard his mother's command, that it is no wonder she finds it so difficult to secure his attention.

Not so with the mother who has complete control over the will of her son. When she tells him to look at A, B, and C, he knows of no way but to attend to them immediately. And so it is as to all her instructions. The child that is under most complete command, is the one most easily taught. It is the more important, then, that we "provoke not our children to wrath," lest we thus impair our authority, and thereby impede our parental instructions.

But the *direct* influence of anger on instruction is much more injurious; for the success of instruction depends much on the state of the child's mind, while receiving it. It is difficult for any one to give good attention to the teachings of others, while his mind is agitated, especially if agitated with anger at his teachers. It is important, therefore, that the minds of our children be kept as placid and pleasant as possible, while we are instructing them. We should be careful, then, to avoid everything that would needlessly irritate, and thus unfit them for heeding our instructions aright.

And attention is still more difficult, when there is a strong dislike both to the teacher and to the lesson taught. Scholars seldom learn well, when they dislike their instructor. Either they set less value on what he teaches, or they are unwilling to gratify him by learning it. We should strive the more to gain and keep the love and esteem of our children, so in order to have them profit the more by our instructions.

But our children have a strong native dislike to much that we need to teach them. And this dislike is much stronger when they are irritated, than when they are in a kind and pleasant mood. We should be very careful, therefore, not to increase this, their aversion, by provoking them to wrath. Moreover, we should present our unwelcome instruction in a way least calculated to wake up their opposition—present them in such language, looks, and tones as are best fitted to show religion in its real loveliness. Yet many a parent is rousing much needless opposition, by the austere manner in which he teaches religious truth. Instead of doing so, they should be so cheerful and affectionate themselves, and speak of religious things in that pleasant manner, which will best show that wisdom's ways "are ways of pleasantness, and all her paths are peace." But more of this in the next discourse.

In conclusion, let me illustrate the importance of the two commands of the text, by contrasting the family in which the children are." provoked to wrath," with the one in which they are "brought up in the nurture and admonition of the Lord." In the former, if the parents command, it is in a sour or crusty manner. If they reprove, it is in harsh language, often interlarded with low or insulting epithets. If they punish, it is with fretfulness or rage. Many commands are given, yet few obeyed; many chastisements threatened, yet few inflicted. The parents literally quarrel with, rather than govern, their children, and have the best of the contest, only as they are the strongest party. And the children, catching the spirit of their parents, command and accuse, threaten and beat each other. Scarcely any kind words are exchanged in the family. Between the railing of the parents and the romping and clamor of the children, you can hardly converse. In some families, you will find all these features; and in not a few, will you find too many of them.[22]

Let us next turn to a more welcome scene. It is the family in which every command is obeyed without delay, murmur, or reserve. And how is such immediate and entire obedience secured? Is it by threatenings, uttered in such loud and terrific tones as makes the child quail at once into compliance? No; not a harsh word is spoken. Is it, then, by such a severe infliction of the rod as drives the child in terror or in pain to submission? No; not a stripe has been given. The parent speaks firmly, but affectionately, and that is enough. The child feels it no hardship to obey, for he knows not what it is to disobey. And the "habit" of obedience "has become his second nature." He is saved, therefore, not only from the pain inflicted in reproof and punishment, but from the no little misery which the disobedient child is inflicting on himself all the time that he delays, in surliness and wrath, to do what is commanded him. Where the habit of immediate and complete obedience is early fixed, there is no occasion for anger, scolding, and flogging on the part of parents, nor any for crying, complaint, or anger, on the part of the children. All things move on, therefore, in complete tranquillity and concord. The parents are familiar and affectionate, the children loving and confiding; consequently, there is no room for vexation and strife. We may say of this family, somewhat as was said of that which contrasts with it, that in some households you will find all these features, and in many you will find more or less of them.

How different must be the influences of these two families upon their inmates, and upon society. What a misfortune to be brought up in the former; what a blessing to be brought up in the latter — especially as it is so well fitted to prepare its inmates for usefulness on earth and blessedness in heaven. How important, then, that we keep our children from the pernicious influence of the former, and subject them to the blessed influence of the latter; in other words, that we make our households what they ought to be, by "not provoking our children to wrath, but bringing them up in the nurture and admonition of the Lord."

The motives that urge to this duty are peculiarly powerful. How, as we think of our intimate connection with our children, as we see our own features in their faces, and consider that our own blood is coursing their veins, how can we provoke them by abusive language or other cruel treatment that is needless? While ardent parental love impels us to labor and suffer so much for their temporal welfare, and fills us with anguish to see them exposed to suffering and death, how can we be so regardless of their *spiritual* and *eternal* welfare, as to expose them, through our anger, heedlessness, or false tenderness, to eternal death? Let us rather resolve so to train them, that they shall all belong to "the household of God, both on earth and in heaven."

Deut. vi. 6, 7.

"These words which I command thee this day, shall be in thine heart. And thou shalt teach them diligently unto thy children."

Lecture 6

Parental Instruction

*I*n these words, parents are virtually required to teach their offspring all the duties which they owe to themselves, to their fellow men, and to God. The object of the present discourse is to show, that such instruction should be early and industriously given.

Parental instruction should be given early, for many of those notions and maxims which shape a man's course and character for life, are acquired in early childhood, while he is under the eye and action of his parents. It is of vast importance, therefore, that they be early on the alert to guard him against those that are evil, and imbue him with those that are good. Many of the pernicious notions and habits on which men act through life, they acquire from the conversation and manners of their associates.

Parents should, therefore, be very cautious how they speak and act before their young children, and to what influence, from nurses and companions, they allow them to be exposed. Moreover, as much knowledge of right and wrong may be taught by looks, tones, and actions, and many good habits given through their sympathy and imitativeness, the best influences of the kind should be brought to bear upon them.

I would now speak mainly of oral instruction. It needs to be deferred, for a while, till some knowledge of language is acquired. But such time may be very profitably occupied in modeling the disposition and subduing the will of the child, thus preparing him the better for receiving instruction. For we have seen, that the more quiet his temper, and the more cheerful and complete his obedience are, the more readily and profitably he will listen to the teachings of his parents.

Yet the time for commencing oral instruction is much earlier than many imagine. For the child understands the meaning of words long before he can speak them. Dr. Dick thinks he does it at the age of eight months. Certainly, by the aid of motions, looks, and tones, he can be made to understand many words within the first year. And later than this the parent's instructions should not be delayed. True, his first lessons must be very simple, and relate to what is most familiar to the child; as, for instance, first, what will injure himself, and then, what will injure others. Then from these he can pass, step by step, to those things that are more and more complex and difficult.

That training of the habits and the will which was begun by silent influence and continued by parental authority, should now be confirmed and completed by instruction. And early should the child be taught, not only what conduct, but what feelings, are due to others. Nor should we fail to teach him what God has so often taught us, viz: that the right regard and treatment of others are ultimately best for ourselves.

In order to aid us in the instruction of children, God has given them a very inquisitive disposition. Hence, they are continually asking questions. This disposition should not be repressed by neglect or reproof. Yet many children are in the habit of asking what they need not know, or what they know already; or, of teasing for answers while their parents are talking with others. Such practices should never be allowed, for they are troublesome. But all proper questions should be promptly and cheerfully answered.

Early, too, should the child be taught to avoid those rough and crabbed tones and actions which will be unfavorable to his enjoyment and usefulness in mature life. For what he forms the habit of doing in the family, when a child, he will be likely to practice in society, when a man. But especially should he be taught all of his moral duties.

"Morality," says Dr. Dwight, "begun in truth and advanced in justice, is finished in kindness. The minds of children may be easily rendered kind by a wise cultivation; and by the want of it, will easily become unfeeling and cruel. Children should be taught, the very first moment they are capable of being taught, a lively tenderness for the feelings, the sufferings, and happiness of all beings with whom they are conversant . . . Even a child should be instructed to exercise kindness toward animals, and to shun cruelty, even to an insect. The plunder of birds' nests and the capture of their young, is, in all ordinary cases, an employment fitted only to harden the heart, and prepare it to be insensible to human suffering." He might have put in this category, the practice of setting dogs to fight, shooting harmless birds, pelting other animals, and many like cruelties. But our author continues: "Children should never injure other animals without reproof, solemnly administered . . . All their unkindness to others, which falls within their knowledge, should be strongly and unconditionally reprobated; at the same time, every instance of spontaneous tenderness and beneficence should be strongly commended." *(Dwight's Theology, Sermon III.)*

But the duties of truth and honesty require a fuller notice, for they are most momentous and ennobling virtues; while lying and injustice are most detestable and pernicious vices. And to these vices children show an early and strong propensity. I will not say, as some do, that all this propensity is the result of example, and other external influences. But I must think a vast amount of it is. For as we shall show, in another place, many parents teach their children lying and deceit most industriously, while they should be striving constantly and vigorously to check their native inclination to these vices.

Some little children, like little George Washington, will not lie, even to escape reproof or punishment. And such, like him, will lay the foundation of a virtuous, worthy character. I have known some men noted for integrity and moral worth, who in childhood had been detected in a falsehood, but who, having been faithfully chastised for it, were never known to lie again; while, probably, of all the cheats and liars that now abound, not one of them was properly chastised for falsehoods when young. It is immensely important, then, that children be early and strictly trained to honesty and truth, by instruction enforced by authority. And so, also, with regard to all other duties to our fellow men. If we would have our children become happy and prosperous, useful and worthy members of society, we should train them early in all the moralities of life.

But it is the *duties of religion* in which our children need most instruction; and this kind of instruction, too, should begin very early. Most Christian parents delay it quite too long. It should be commenced before the mind of the child gets preoccupied with false notions, and while the heart is most tender, and, therefore, most susceptible of good impressions. Parents succeed in making their young children understand their instructions about worldly things. And if they would he equally skillful and persevering in trying to make them understand religious truth, they might impart to them a vast amount of most important information. We make our children understand, very early, that we love to have them act right, and that we are displeased, and must punish them if they do wrong. And from this we can proceed to teach them, of their "Father in heaven;" that he is angry with us, his children, when we do wrong, and must punish us, unless we leave our sins. We make them understand, too, that they should love and obey us, their parents on earth. And from this we can proceed to teach them that they should love and obey their "Father in heaven," who gives them life and all its blessings; consequently, that it is very wicked not to love so good a being. Thence, we can proceed, from step to step, through all the essential duties of religion. And such instruction is especially needful to those who have to leave home while young, whether for service, for apprenticeship, or for school. For they need to be strongly fortified by early education, in order to resist the evil influences that will then throng around them.

Many of the facts, precepts, and principles that are taught in the bible, may be learned by the child, before he can read the holy records. Parents can *translate* them, so to speak, into the child's dialect, and thus enable him to understand them. Many a child has learned, in this way, more of the bible before he could read it, than many an adult reader has. And the truths thus early taught will make the deepest impression, and be the best remembered. How much better, then, to store his mind with these truths than with the stories of witches, ghosts, hobgoblins, with "raw heads and bloody bones," by which he becomes so frightened as to be always afraid when alone in the dark.

Some, I wish I could say many, parents help their children while thus young, to commit to memory those excellent hymns which Dr. Watts, Jane Taylor, and others have written for infant minds, to store them with important religious truths. And how much better this than to teach those silly, sickening doggerels that are taught by many a mother. How long shall these nonsensical, disgusting things be employed in training to giddiness, frivolity, and "fun," those children that are pledged to be "brought up in the nurture and admonition of the Lord."

But as early as possible, should the child be taught to read the bible, and to learn its truths by himself. Nor has he, as many suppose, such a strong native aversion to it as will render it very difficult to make him study it. Much of the aversion to it is the result of parental mismanagement. Some require their children to read the bible as a punishment; and there is no surer way to make them hate it. They should rather be allowed to read it as *a privilege*. If we would begin early, and manage wisely, we can waken our children to a deep interest in many facts recorded in God's word. If we were to speak of them as "the pretty and wonderful stories" found in the bible, they would soon be on the hunt for them. Children delight in the marvelous. And what more wonderful, than the miraculous events and extraordinary characters which the word of God describes. I have

known my sons, while young and impenitent, to be so much interested in bible narratives, that when, in the course of family reading,
we entered on one of them, they would return to it as soon as prayer
was over, nor cease till they had read the whole of it.

The *precepts,* also, and the *doctrines* of the bible, should be early
taught; and, first of all, the Ten Commandments and the Savior's
Golden Rule. Early, too, should the Shorter Catechism be taught. I
believe a better summary of scripture doctrines cannot be found. I
know its language is better suited to a student in divinity than to a
child. But this defect, if it be one, can be easily remedied by parents.
They can simplify, explain, and illustrate its meaning; thus rendering
it at once more easy and interesting. But, even if the child is compelled to the task of committing to memory what he does not understand, the labor is not lost. Like the student in *grammar,* who has at
first to commit to memory much in which he sees neither use nor
meaning, he may find, in the end, much meaning, profit, and pleasure. But many have not found these benefits till late in life, when
they have burst at once upon them through the converting grace of
God. And then they have been surprised that, they could remember
the language of the Catechism so distinctly, and see its meaning so
vividly.

And there are many other books that should be in the hands of
children. Time was, when "Pilgrim's Progress," "Janeway's Tokens,"
and "Watt's and Taylor's Hymns for Infant Minds," were about all
the books that were fit for their perusal. But, since the days of Sabbath schools, a vast amount of juvenile literature of salutary character has been provided. And parents should see that their children are
supplied with such books as are best suited to improve their minds
and hearts. What a pity, that instead of these, there should be found
in the families of professed Christians such contemptible trash as
"Mother Goose," "Mother Hubbard," "The Old Dame, and her Silver
Sixpence," "Tom Thumb," and a score of others like them.

But many a parent seems to think, that as he sends his children to Sabbath school, he is absolved from the duty of teaching them at home. Yet the Sabbath school teacher is only his assistant, not his substitute; an aid that should encourage him to do more, not less. For what he does, will benefit his children the more by means of the Sabbath school. He should teach his children much that is not, and perhaps cannot, be taught in the school. He should, moreover, aid his children in getting their lessons, and see that they go and recite them. If he cannot become a teacher himself, he should at least visit the school, in order to encourage both his children and their teachers. And if the Commandments and Catechism are not taught in the school, they should be the more thoroughly taught at home. He should, moreover, require them to read the bible by course, and encourage them to inquire into its meaning, faithfully and affectionately answering their questions, till it can be said of them, as of Timothy, that "from a child he had known the scriptures that are able to make him wise unto salvation."[23]

But the proper matter and amount of parental instruction is not enough. Much depends on the manner and spirit in which it is given. It should always be given in an earnest and serious manner, but never in a sour or sanctimonious one, much less in a severe, censorious one; for it will impede the child's progress in divine truth, and make the impression on his mind that religion is cheerless and unlovely. Many parents err quite egregiously in this respect. They need, therefore, to be cautioned the more earnestly to always be affectionate and cheerful when speaking on the subject of religion, so as to leave the impression that it is amiable and delightful, and, therefore, that the way to be *happy* is to *be good*. Much more needs to be said on this subject, and much more I hope to say in another place.

But, says the skeptic, "Let the child alone, till he is old enough to judge for himself what religious opinions to adopt." Yet a more absurd sentiment could scarcely be urged. If it be valid as to religion, it must be valid as to all secular affairs. I would, therefore, ask the infidel, and all others who urge this sentiment, (for it is urged by many who would not like to be classed with the rejectors of revelation,) Why not carry out this notion into all the concerns of life? Why teach your children to read? or why send them to school? Why not wait till they are old enough to judge for themselves, whether they had better learn to read, write, and "cypher"? For some insist, you know, that mankind would be better without the knowledge of letters, as it makes men proud and dishonest. They, therefore, boast of having never gone to school, to learn counterfeiting and other knaveries. And how do you know but your children would "think just so, too," if you did not bias their minds by early education? It is not probable that one in ten of your children would have any learning, if left to themselves.

And why teach your children that it is wicked to lie and steal, rob or murder? It may be that, if left to themselves till old enough to judge for themselves, they would think it best for them to live as others do, by lying and theft, violence and bloodshed. Then, why not leave them, unbiased by early education, to take their own way?

Do you say, "This would be dangerous to them, as they would be liable, if left to themselves, to take to wrong courses; and as we are their natural guardians, it is our duty to warn them from the wrong, and urge them to the right way?" All this is most evidently true. And it is as evidently and emphatically true in relation to the principles of religion. You learn not only from the bible, but from your own experience and observation, that your children, like all others, are prone to wrong opinions and practices; and that, therefore, they need to be guarded against them by instruction and restraint. If, then, you know "the better way," it is your duty to teach your offspring to walk in it.

And this infidel sentiment is as much at war with philosophy as with revelation. It is well known by those who understand the laws of mind, that the younger the child is; the more easily his opinions and habits are formed, and the more firmly they are fixed. Consequently, the earlier he embraces an error, or commences an evil course, the more difficult it is to turn him from it. So, on the other hand, the earlier the truth is implanted and the course of duty begun, the more probable it is that they will be abiding.

How evident, then, that you should urge upon your children, as early as possible, the adoption of right principles and right practices, especially as the longer they are left to themselves, the surer they will be to go wrong through life. What! would you suffer your sons to follow the multitude in the use of *tobacco* or *alcohol,* in hopes that "when they come to years of discretion," they will see their folly, and forsake it? No; you would say, "The power of example and custom is so strong, that I fear my sons would get their taste and habit so confirmed that they would never break away from them." And if the danger is so great in cases where the native taste is opposed, (as in the case of tobacco and alcohol,) how much greater where the native inclination is strongly in favor of error and sin? As, then, the consequences of evil are infinite, it is unspeakably important that right instruction be given, early and earnestly.

Nor will such instruction hinder the child's judging correctly of religion, when he does arrive at maturity. It will rather aid him to judge the more correctly. Such instruction will exercise his intellect, thus invigorating and improving it. It will also give him more information as to the evidences, nature, and tendencies of religion. He can, therefore, judge more understandingly. And though the habit of believing it true may somewhat incline him to continue of that opinion, yet it will not overbalance his native inclination to reject it. And while the counter influences are so nearly poised, it will be less difficult to judge correctly. How absurd the notion, then, that young children should be left without religious instruction

And this notion is as pernicious as it is preposterous. For, if fathers and mothers will not teach their children, Satan will. Something they will be learning continually. And it is for parents to say, whether that something shall be good or evil, and whether it shall lead their

offspring to "glory and honor," or to "shame and everlasting contempt." He, then, who neglects the proper religious instruction of his
children, is inflicting upon them an infinite wrong, as it leaves them
so liable to incalculable evil, both in this life and the life to come.
While, on the other hand, if he would instruct them as fully and as
affectionately as he ought, they would usually be converted in youth,
live happy and useful lives, and be finally saved with an "eternal
salvation." But on this point I hope to dwell at large in a future
discourse.

Ps. 19. 12.

*"Who can understand his errors?
cleanse thou me from secret fault."*

Lecture 7

Parental Mismanagement

*I*n these words two things are virtually taught. One is, that is difficult to know our own faults. The other is, that it is desirable to have our faults pointed out, in order to avoid them. And these things are emphatically true as to the management of parents in the government and instruction of children. I shall take the opportunity, therefore, to notice some important errors in parental training. Some of them have been already glanced upon. But it is needful to dwell more upon them, and to place them, together with others, in the same discourse, that the reader may more easily refer to them afterward. They are such as I have often noticed during the thirty-eight years of my ministry, in which I have visited twenty states and several thousand families. My readers should judge for themselves, which of these errors are their own, and consider the importance of immediately avoiding them.

These errors would all be prevented by the proper exercise of Love, Consideration, and Firmness. The proper exercise of love to their children, joined with consideration, would prompt parents to ascertain how they ought to train them. And this, with a proper amount of firmness, would cause them to act accordingly. And the same *love, consideration* and *firmness* are needful, in order to search out and correct the errors of the past.

Many err in always speaking to their children in words and tones of *authority*. We should command only when it becomes necessary. Having gained a full control over our children, it is better generally to say to them, "I wish you to do this;" or, "Will you do that?" For this gentleness of manner would secure the more love from them, and give the more force to our words, when we do command. While, if we are continually and sternly bidding them, it will have the same effect upon them that the farmer has upon his team by chiding and lashing them incessantly. They soon care nothing about it.

And some go still further. They allow their children the habit of always speaking authoritatively and harshly, not only to each other, but to themselves. Nothing is asked—everything is demanded. And this tends to make them of a rough, despotic disposition. If we would have our children sweet and amiable in heart and behavior, we must not permit them to speak thus sternly to others.

Many err in punishing the child in such a way as to show that their object is to give vent to their anger, or at best to express their displeasure at his ill conduct. Whereas, they should tell him their object is his good, and should show in their manner the sincerity of their declaration. Many are, and more should be, in the habit of spending considerable time with the child alone, seriously, yet affectionately, admonishing him respecting his fault, showing him the need of chastising him for it, and praying with him for a blessing on the chastisement. Not a few have done so with the happiest results. For their children have yielded at once, and shown a great change for the better, ever afterward. But if they do not yield at first, the punishment should be continued till they do submit, show sorrow, and seek forgiveness, and not be left, as many are, to bellow and storm; for this would only make them worse. Solomon said, "Chasten thy son, while there is hope, and *let not thy soul spare for his crying.*"[24] And he might have said, *spare not till he ceases crying.* For outcries under the rod are usually the ebullitions of anger, that cease when he is completely subdued. Yet when he submits, he should be affectionately and fondly received. But many parents taunt and twit him, afterward, about it, either in anger or in sport—both of which sadly impair the reformatory influence of punishment.

Many err in fostering in their children the taste and habit of *destructiveness.* It begins, generally, in tearing flowers, papers, and books; next, perhaps, in breaking or whittling other things at home; and, afterward, in defacing seats in school or church. And it tends to make them unsafe and mischievous, reckless and wasteful. In later life they will probably be the more careless of their own property and that of others. Both their own welfare and the public good require that such a habit be prevented. We should, therefore, teach our children that it is wrong, and should restrain them from it.

The error of some is, that when their child is doing wrong, they turn away and pretend not to notice him. This they do to avoid the trouble of correcting him. But though minor offenses may be overlooked, serious ones never should. These parents seem to suppose that, in such, cases, the child thinks he is not detected in his wrong doing. But he should rather be taught that he cannot escape detection. And if he is not corrected for a wrong act, he will be the more emboldened to repeat that and others of the kind, thinking either that he shall not be detected, or that though detected, he shall not be reproved.

The error of other parents is that they educate their children to be *fickle* and *fastidious, restless* and *arrogant.* They do it by giving them too many toys or other gratifications at once, or changing them too often. They do it by asking, at table or elsewhere, "Will you have some of this? Will you have some of that?" And it is soon found that they are hard to please. As the child hardly knows what to choose, the father places something on his plate; but it is met with a flash or explosion of displeasure not a little annoying to others at the table. Such a child will clamor and storm if he is not the first to be waited on. And he will probably become self-important and whimsical, arrogant and willful, and finally fixed in these habits, perhaps for life. Such a treatment will be apt, also, to impair the child's appetite and health. For, he will probably choose such food as is most unfit for him. His parents ought to know what is best for him, and to decide accordingly. And when his own choice is least consulted, he will be most easily satisfied, most contented and happy.

The chief aim of many fond parents is to delight their children. Hence, their profusion of toys, trinkets, and other "pretties," the nuts, candies, etc., for early childhood. Hence, their many ornaments and fine dresses, amusements and parties of pleasure, for more advanced life, and their contrivances to make play of everything. These things tend to make children giddy and pleasure-loving, careless and impatient of labor; thus unfitting them for the sober and needful concerns of life. When young, they will read nothing, unless it be amusing stories; when older, nothing but novels, romances, and the like trashy and useless productions. And, through life, they will probably be on chase for pleasures, and thereby become comparatively useless to themselves and their fellow men.

Children should be trained to *usefulness,* not pleasure. Rather, they should be taught to find their highest enjoyment in acts of justice and benevolence. They should, for this purpose, be early accustomed to regular times of earnest thought and active employment. It is, however, the prominence and excess of amusements and pleasures that I would condemn, not a moderate share of them. Much less is it sadness or depression that I would recommend, but a sobriety consistent with cheerfulness.

But many who mismanage thus, are doing it not so much for their children's pleasure as for their own. They make mere playthings of them. Of such a parent Babington says, "What would he say of any one who threw about his gold repeater as if it were a ball, or sported with his wife's jewels as if they were marbles? And yet his own folly is infinitely greater. The creatures whom he places in such danger for his sport, are infinitely more precious than gold which perisheth; and pearls and diamonds are worthless compared with them." (*Practical View*, p. 48.)

Many err in such management of their children as makes them *rough, disrespectful, contradictious,* and *fault-finding, self-conceited* and *indelicate.* They make them rough and rude by the influence of their homes. In their houses there is the continual clatter and clangor of a machine shop. Every movement is a rush. Every step is a stamp, and every word a vociferation. The shovel and tongs, the dishes and the doors, are made to contribute their portion of noise. And in such homes it is seen, that the children are seldom of a soft and quiet disposition.[25] And to see the influence of quiet families, look among our friends, the Quakers.

Children are made rough and boisterous, also, by being permitted to engage much in rude and noisy sports. Many are indulged in loud talking and singing, and other annoying efforts to gain the notice of visitors. It is strange that their parents do not see how much they are injuring their children, as well as disturbing others and disgracing themselves, by such allowances. To render them easy and agreeable to society when grown, they must be made to behave quietly and respectfully while young. But many permit them to be so noisy and boisterous in their plays, both at home and in the streets, as to disturb all that are near. And they plead for it, that it will make their children more robust and active. But plays far less vociferous and violent would better fit them for the activities of life, rendering them at the same time more acceptable and thus more useful to others.

Some parents make their children disrespectful to others, by permitting them to be irreverent to themselves. The young child is allowed, and even taught, to be pert and mischievous, for the amusement of his parents—to pull their hair, slap their faces, and call them ill names. A more odious impropriety is permitting him to contradict his parents, and still more so, to flatly refuse obedience. It shocks me, most painfully, to hear a child say to his mother, "I won't." How any parent can endure to receive such a reply, is to me a mystery. And how can it be expected that one who treats his father or mother thus, will be respectful to others?

Parents make their children contradictious and fault-finding by their own example, and by allowing them in the early practice of disputing and censuring each other, or worse, of disputing and censuring themselves. Brothers and sisters should be allowed, and even encouraged, in mildly and affectionately correcting each other's errors and faults. Few practices are more amiable. But that sharp and ill-natured manner of doing it which prevails in many families, is very unlovely. It seems to be prompted by a spirit of malevolence, or at best, by an ambition of acuteness in spying out the errors of others. And the continual practice of it has an insensible, yet powerful, effect on the permanent temper and habits of the household. Parents should, therefore, strive by example, authority, and instruction to prevent it.

Some make their children self-conceited, by making them too conspicuous in the family. The young master must be introduced to the guests as ceremoniously as any of the household. And then, the visitors must be duly informed that he is a very uncommon child, by being told his smart tricks, and especially, as the smartest of all, his roguish ones;[26] all of which the child notices as much as the visitors do, and probably relishes it much more. For they may not exactly like to be thus indirectly told, that this child is much smarter than their own. Nor will the child fail to get the impression, that he is of much consequence; an impression which he will be likely to carry through life. And if a great share of conversation with him, and before him, be, as it too often is, in praise of his beauty, fine dress, or the like, there is no calculating how much is thus done to inflate him with vanity and pride.

Some regard to personal appearance ought to be cultivated, such as cleanliness of person, and neatness of dress; for they will render our children more agreeable and thus more useful to others. And there are two other ornaments that should have especial attention, as they are no less valuable in themselves, or acceptable to others, than the beauties of feature and form, while at the same time they are less liable to inflate with self-consequence. They are, sweetness of tones, and gentleness of manners. And these should be taught early, as it will be easier for the teacher and the taught.

But it is wonderful in what harsh tones and incorrect pronunciation many allow their children to talk, thinking, if they think at all, that they must be corrected at some future day. And thus they confirm bad habits that will be overcome with difficulty, if ever; whereas, if they would teach them, from the beginning, to pronounce properly, and to speak in sweet inflections and mellow tones, they would give them a grace more acceptable to good society, than all the trinkets that they could pile upon them. But instead of doing so, they actually mislead the child by speaking to him in "baby-talk;" and then confirm his faults by mimicking him in a way that makes him think, as they themselves seem to do, that they are beauties, and not blemishes.

The most that parents can do in teaching agreeable manners, is to correct what is coarse, awkward, and affected; to point the child to good examples; to inculcate, in regard to manners, as well as personal appearance, the saying, trite though it be, "Handsome they who handsome do;" and to persuade him that he needs much more precious ornaments than the tailor, manteau-maker, or jeweler can furnish him.

Many make their children indelicate, by appearing before them in an unbecoming manner, or by speaking to or before them in low, filthy language. It is a fact, that many who wish to be considered decent people, act or speak very indecently before their young children; either vainly supposing it will not be noticed, or not thinking at all of the effect of it. They do it, also, by allowing their children to act and speak unbecomingly among themselves, or to associate with those who do. How often have children received a taint of moral impurity from an obscene anecdote, which they were thought too young to notice, a taint whose influence lasted for life.

The error of others is, that they teach their children to be *sordid* and *grudging, passionate* and *revengeful.* When they wish one to do something that is disagreeable, (to take medicine, for instance,) and he refuses, they provoke him to it by exciting his selfishness. They say to him, "Well, if you won't drink this, sister shall have it." And sometimes they add, "Drink it quick, before sister gets it." And then down goes the dose, just to keep another from having it. Here, then, is one of the most hateful human passions deliberately called into action. And the more it is exercised, the more it is strengthened and confirmed. No, worse; the child is indirectly taught that he does well to be thus sordid and grudging. Nor are the occasions few in which many parents call out the evil affections of their children as induce-ments to obey; whereas, obedience from such motives is really no obedience, but the hurtful gratification of a hateful passion.

Many teach their children to be passionate and revengeful in ways like these: The child bumps his head against a chair; and the mother, to hush his outcries, says, "Did the naughty chair hurt my baby? We'll whip it." And then she falls to beating it, most condignly. If he is hushed by these means, it is because he is gratified at the sup-posed sufferings of the chair; that is, by the gratification of anger or revenge. We might laugh at this silly means of the mother, if the injury which she inflicts upon her child did not forbid our levity. She does him no little injury by exciting and thus confirming these pas-sions, and by indirectly teaching him that they are proper.

Or, the child is in the arms of an elder sister, crying lustily from sheer anger. His mother takes him, at length, and says, "Did they abuse my boy? They will not do so anymore." And then she deals out upon the innocent girl a pretended chastisement. To say nothing of the sin of falsehood in this case, the mother teaches her child to vent a wicked vengeance against the innocent, and thereby makes him the more irritable and vindictive.

Lastly, many teach their children to *lie* and *deceive*. They do it in many ways, and with lamentable industry. They do it mainly by lying to them, or by lying before them. Many lie to their children in false statements, threatenings, or promises. In some families many such falsehoods are told every day. Go where there is much scolding — consequently, little government — and you will find it is so. In such families, the child is told, "You won't have your breakfast, depend upon it, till you wash your face." But, before long, the smutty urchin comes to the table undisturbed. Soon after, he does something wrong, and is told, "I will whip you, as true as you are born, if you ever do that again." But, though he soon repeats the fault, the promised chastisement never comes. Sometimes the child cries to go to town, or elsewhere, but is put off with the promise that he shall go "next time." Yet many a "next time" comes before the oft-repeated promise is fulfilled. And often does he cry for something that is present, but the parent hides it, and says it is gone. Or, he is told, "You won't have it;" but he teases or bawls after it till the parent says, "There, take it, and stop your noise." Often, too, is he told the hen will pick him, or the snake bite, the cow hook, or the horse kick him, or worse, that the bug-bears (booggers) or spooks will catch him. I have no doubt that many parents tell their children ten thousand such falsehoods in a year.

Some are in the habit of threatening the same punishment ten times over, without inflicting it at all. They even threaten what they never intend to inflict, and what their children do not believe they will inflict—indeed, what they would be shocked to have them believe; such as "skinning them alive," "cutting their heads off," and the like. If a visitor comes in, they will say, "This man has a sharp knife; and if you don't behave, he will cut off your ears." This they will say of their physician or minister, thus putting them so much in fear of him, that it is difficult for him to do them any good. And many, moreover, will lie to others in the hearing of their children, either telling what their children know to be false, or boasting before them how they have deceived others. Now, all these things are lies, and nothing but lies. And in these "I speak that I do know, and testify that I have seen," in thousands of instances.

What, then, must be the tendency of so much parental falsehood, but to teach their children lying and deceit. As children are such imitative beings, and inclined to "go astray as soon as they be born, speaking lies," it would be strange, indeed, if they did not copy such examples. What is there to hinder them from doing what their "dear, good parents" are doing so constantly, and what is so congenial to themselves? A great share of that detestable class called liars and deceivers, have undoubtedly been made such by this kind of parental training; and untold evils have thence resulted. It might, also, be shown, that many parents educate their children to falsehood by not properly punishing them for it, and even by requiring them to lie. But on this I have not time to dwell.

While the greatest evil resulting from such treatment is that it leads the child to lying and deception, there are others that should not be overlooked. One is, that the child thus deceived will not believe his parents when they do tell him the truth. They tell him, for instance, that the cakes or the nuts are all eaten up. But he has so often detected them in falsehood, that he cannot rely upon their word. They have, therefore, not only to repeat the assertion often and positively, but to let him run his hand into their pockets, or search the closets, to convince him; whereas, if they had always told him the truth, he would never have doubted their word.

But the other evil resulting from this treatment is much more serious. It is its ruinous influence on parental authority. How can a child *"honor* his father and mother" as much as is needful to filial obedience, if he cannot trust their word? And how can he stand in proper fear of chastisement, when it is so often threatened without infliction? "Mother," said a little girl to her foster-parent (from whom I had the account) "Mother, you shouldn't tell Jimmie you will whip him, unless you do it; for he don't believe you. I told him t'other day you would whip him, if he did such a thing, for you said you would. 'No she won't,' said he, 'she has often told me she would, but she has never done it.' " And this is only one out of a multitude of cases, in which I have known this practice to ruin parental authority. Yes, fathers and mothers, you must give up lying to your children, or give up your ability to govern them. More; you must cease lying to them, or contribute fearfully to their temporal and eternal ruin.

I entreat all parents to consider how important it is that they abstain from all the errors that have now been noticed—important to the community, to themselves, and especially to their children; and how unwise and wicked those must be who are conscious of having been guilty of these errors, and yet carelessly or deliberately persist in them. Let all parents consider that their children are the most precious objects of their care. Let the father feel, that among all his affairs, in the field or shop, the study or the store, he has no concern of more importance than the training of his household. And let the mother say of her offspring, as Cornelia did, "These are my jewels." And let her so train them that they shall be jewels, indeed jewels that shall richly adorn herself on earth, and stud the crown of her Savior in heaven.

Prov. xxii. 6.

"Train up a child in the way he should go;
and when he is old he will not depart from it."

Lecture 8

Childhood Conversion

The way in which a child should go, can be no other than the path of true piety. And to train him to that path, can be no less than causing him to become a Christian in his childhood. I see not how the text can be made to mean any less. It cannot mean that he is in the way of religion already, and needs only to make progress in it. For, he is "by nature a child of wrath, even as others." He must, then, be converted, to enter "the way he should go," and converted early, or he cannot be trained in it during his childhood. And how is he to be converted? Not by a recuperative power of his own, nor by any sanctifying influence lodged in his parents; but by "the renewing of the Holy Ghost."[27] And yet the change is to be effected through the instrumentality of parental training. He is to be cleansed from his original corruption, just as the adult Christian is cleansed from his remaining corruptions; that is, he is to "purify his soul by obeying the truth through the Spirit."[28] It is by yielding to the commands and teachings of his parents, through the influence of the Spirit, that he is born again.

But as many are acting evidently under the notion that Childhood Conversion is impossible, (a notion which Christ rebuked in saying, "Suffer little children to come unto me, for of such is the kingdom of God,") I propose to show, that under proper parental training, it is both *a possible and a probable attainment.*

The possibility of early conversion is virtually taught in the text. It requires the child to be brought up in a way which involves regeneration. And as God never commands a positive impossibility, we must infer that the early conversion which he requires the parent to

secure, is in its nature attainable. And the same thing is taught in the
apostolic version of the text; that is, the command to bring up our
children in the "nurture and admonition of the Lord."[29] It is likewise
taught thus indirectly in what God said of the parental faithfulness
of Abraham: "I know him, that he will command his children and his
household after him; and they shall keep the way of the Lord, to do
justice and judgment."[30] And as he "was a man of like passions with
ourselves," what he did, other parents can do. And by the Abrahamic
or Family Covenant, they are positively required to do it.[31]

The possibility of childhood conversion is taught, likewise, in the
following declarations of Solomon: "Foolishness" (that is sin) "is
bound in the heart of a child; but the rod of correction" (or proper
parental discipline) "will drive it far from him." "Withhold not
correction from the child: for if thou beatest him with the rod, *he
shall not die.*" (That is, he shall not be lost.) "Thou shalt beat him
with the rod, and shalt deliver his soul from hell." "The rod and
reproof give wisdom," (i. e., true religion.) "Correct thy son, and he
shall give thee rest; yea, he shall give delight to thy soul;"[32] (a "rest"
and "delight," evidently, which nothing but the child's piety could
give.) And does not the declaration of Christ, that we must receive
the kingdom of God as a little child, furnish a cumulative proof of the
same?[33]

The possibility of early conversion is also proven by many modern
facts. Numerous cases are recorded, in which children must have
been born again at a very early age. The daughter of Dr. Doddridge,
Dinah Doudney, Phebe Bartlet, Nathan W. Dickerman, John Mooney
Mead, and many others in our own land, are among the number, as
may be seen by consulting our Sabbath school libraries. And they
occur, perhaps, more frequently in Scottish and Moravian churches
than in others.[34]

And why may not the child as well be converted under parental
training, as the adult under the preaching of the gospel? Say not, that
the child cannot know enough to be born again. For no one knows

exactly how much knowledge is necessary to a change of heart, much less, that the child cannot receive that amount. Persons are converted with very little divine knowledge, especially among the heathen. And that little may be rendered so simple, that children can understand it. For they have all the mental and moral capacities and powers of adults; consequently, all their susceptibilities. Much of the bible, by the simplicity of its language and its poetic images, is adapted to the youthful mind. Yes; and many young Sabbath school scholars have more religious knowledge, than many adult Christians. And they would have much more, if their parents did their duty. Moreover, children are more susceptible of good impressions than when they are more aged and hardened.

Thus, the possibility of regeneration in childhood is shown by the bible, and by modern facts, while nothing can be found either in the word of God, or in the nature of the case, that even seems to teach the contrary. Is it not strange, then, that so many parents assume it in practice, if not in theory, as an undoubted truth, that their offspring cannot, be converted in early youth!

But we may have to go much farther. We have yet to see, that under proper parental training, childhood conversion is not only a possible, but a *probable* event. I am far from maintaining that all parents who give their children any kind or amount of religious culture, will probably secure their salvation. I hold, only, that if the right kind is given in a proper manner, and to a certain amount, it will probably be successful. Those who fail, therefore, should charge their want of success to want of faithfulness; while those who train their children in all respects properly, may confidently expect them to be early renewed and finally saved; that according to the teaching of the text, they will walk in the path of piety while young, and not forsake it when old, but be "kept by the power of God through faith unto salvation."

It is true, that conversions among young children appear to be rare. And for this several reasons may be given. One is, that such are not apt to be noticed; for they are not so much looked for, nor so conspicuous as adult conversions. Yet many of our most exemplary Christians must have been renewed in early childhood, for they could never recollect when their renovation took place. That eminent saint, Richard Baxter, was such. And he was once in great trouble, fearing he was not a Christian, because he knew not when he became one. So it was with that eminent missionary, Dr. Scudder. And I believe, that many misdate their spiritual birth, thinking it took place in adult life, when they had (as many Christians have) a season of great darkness, succeeded by unusual light and joy; whereas, they had had the like feelings, though fainter ones, far back in childhood. Many rely too exclusively on the marvelous experiences of adult conversions, and, therefore, regard those Christians who cannot tell of undergoing such a manifest and wonderful change, as graceless formalists.

Still it is a lamentable truth, that comparatively few children become early pious. But this is fully accounted for, as the result of parental neglect. Few are even seeking the early conversion of their children, and fewer still are seeking it aright. It is a deplorable fact, that many, reputed to be very pious and zealous Christians, have very irreligious children. Yet this should lead us to doubt, not the wisdom and efficacy of the training which God commands, but whether these parents are in fact as pious and zealous as they are supposed to be. The fact argues defect somewhere. It did so in the case of Eli, when "his sons made themselves vile, and he restrained them not." It did so in Paul's view respecting bishops and deacons. For he tells us none are fit for such offices who do not "rule their own houses well." It must, then, be no small defect in private Christians.

Some parents, who are regarded as patterns of piety abroad, are found to have certain dispositions and habits at home that make them bad rulers and instructors of their households. They manifest their religion, if not too much abroad, at least too little in the family. They are particularly deficient in the government and instruction of their children, and in prayer for their salvation. And they set before them sad examples of passion and worldliness, if not of more presumptuous sins; which things prejudice their children against religion all the more, if these parents have much reputation for piety abroad.

And some parents, who are otherwise estimable, seem far more thorough and skillful in everything else, than in the training of their children. They are either too lax or too severe; or, they are too inconsiderate, impulsive, or inconsistent. Either they are not sufficiently simple in their religious instructions, or not sufficiently kind or earnest in their persuasions. Or, they discourage their children from efforts to do right, by telling them they can do nothing to purpose, till they have a new heart; whereas, they should leave them to discover it by their own experience. They should rather teach them that, as they can never be made to pray acceptably so long as they neglect to pray at all, so they should not expect to be renewed, till they try to "*purify themselves* by obeying the truth through the spirit."

The fault of others is, that they do not create the right kind of "domestic atmosphere." For the spiritual, as well as the physical welfare of our children depends much on the air which they inhale. And to create the right atmosphere, we must show in our families, by all our words and actions, that we regard religion not only as our chief duty, but as our chief *interest* and *enjoyment.* But how many act as if the world were "the chief concern," both of themselves and of their children. They are all anxiety, and effort, and care, when disease or pain assail the bodies of their offspring. But how little care they for that "leprosy of sin" which pollutes, and pains, and perils the soul. They are eager to improve their minds and manners, while the priceless soul is forgotten. They spare no expense in dress and ornaments to make their children "appear respectable" among men, but do little or nothing to secure them that wedding garment which they need for "the marriage supper of the Lamb." And they make very great exertions to give them "a good start in the world." But ah! how little they are doing to move them to take the first step in the way to heaven. This fact, then, that so few are converted in childhood, is no proof against our proposition, *that under proper parental training, childhood conversion would be a probable and certain event.*

We will now consider the proofs by which this proposition is supported. I give you,

1. The adaptation and efficiency of the means appointed. These means are comprised, as we have seen, in proper parental training. And we shall see, they are well adapted to accomplish the end in view. All are well aware that the evil influences and instructions of a parent are powerful to lead his child astray. Good influence and instruction, then, must have an opposite and powerful tendency. And all allow that the preaching of the gospel is well adapted to secure the conversion of adults; that though in itself alone it is insufficient, on account of native depravity, still its tendency is to resist that depravity; and thus to lead men to salvation. So, also, in regard to example. It is generally admitted, that the holy lives of minister and people give his preaching much additional power. And it is believed that many a man has been won to truth and godliness more by the examples of some consistent saints, than by all the arguments that have reached them from press or pulpit.

Now, both these influences are combined to the best advantage in right parental nurture. And, if they are so effective on adults, they must be more so on children. For the latter are not so much "hardened through the deceitfulness of sin," not so preoccupied with wrong notions, nor so fixed in evil habits; neither are they so disturbed by negative influences, while under parental training, as are adults under the preaching of the gospel.

One great hindrance to the success of the gospel is, that it is heard so seldom—once or twice a week, perhaps—while, during the interval, the world comes in with its numberless disturbances to obliterate the lessons of the Sabbath. And another powerful hindrance is, the influence of evil examples. Adults are usually surrounded with more evil than good ones. But children of Christian families can be mainly kept from these pernicious influences; and that, too, where they can have "precept upon precept," and "line upon line;" not "here a little and there a little," but much, daily and hourly. If, then, the parental teachings and examples are as correct as they should be, the result must be great and good, especially if associated with right parental government.

God sometimes exceeds his promises, by converting the children of unfaithful parents. But, with such exceptions, faithfulness measures success. At least, the case cannot be found in which parents have been perfect in the training of their child, and yet have failed to secure his salvation. As God has appointed parental training as a means for the child's conversion, it cannot be that he would allow the perfect use of it to prove a failure; for he never said to the seed of Jacob, "Seek ye me in vain."[35] And this brings us to the other and main proof of our proposition, that under right treatment *childhood conversion is probable.* It is,

2. The promises and declarations of scripture respecting those that are "brought up in the nurture and admonition of the Lord." And foremost of these, stands the promise of God, first to Abraham, and afterward to Isaac and Jacob, "In him and his seed all the families of the earth shall be blessed."[36] This promise was made to him, as we have seen, because he would "command his children and his household after him."[37] And it is a promise not only to him, but to all who have the like faith, and who therefore train their children as he did his, "to keep the way of the Lord;"[38] a virtual promise, then, that all those who bring up their children fully "in the nurture and admonition of the Lord," shall secure their salvation. And this is confirmed by many other promises of God to bless his saints, together with their children.[39] But such a promise would yield a parent but poor encouragement, if his utmost efforts to train them thus would probably be fruitless.

Several passages which have been already quoted to prove

conversion in childhood *possible,* as fully prove it *probable.* The first
that I would quote, again, is the text, "Train up a child in the way he
should go, and when he is old he will not depart from it." It is here
implied, that a child, rightly trained, not only *can,* but positively *will,*
walk in a way implying conversion, and will persevere in it for life.

The other passages are the following: "Foolishness is bound in the
heart of a child; but the rod of correction will drive it far from him."
"Withhold not correction from the child; for if thou beatest him with
the rod, he shall not die. Thou shalt beat him with the rod, and shalt
deliver his soul from hell." "Correct thy son, and he shall give thee
rest; yea, he shall give delight to thy soul."[40]

These passages assert, not only the *possible,* but the positive conversion of those children that are faithfully trained. They assert that
the rod, which I understand to be the emblem both of instruction
and government, will drive sin from the heart of a child, and will so
fully reform him that he will give "rest" and "delight" to the pious
parent's anxious soul; and that the change thus wrought will be a
saving one, for they teach that the child "shall not die, but his soul
shall be saved from hell." And will any one dare to say, There is *no
probability* that these positive promises will be fulfilled? If the discipline were *perfect,* would not the conversion be sure? If we came up
fully to the conditions of the promise, would God fail to fulfill it?

But though this discipline be imperfect, there is still a probability
of success, proportioned to the degree of our faithfulness. For all
parental nurture will benefit the *child,* as the preaching of the gospel
does the *adult,* in proportion to its amount and excellence. And the
nearer this nurture approaches perfection, the nearer does the probability of its success approach to certainty. Here, then, is great encouragement to parental fidelity.

And there are two other encouragements to such faithfulness,
which are not entirely out of place here. One is, that though the child
does not become pious early, there is a probability of his future
conversion, in proportion to his culture in childhood. Many who are

born again in maturity, and some in old age, are brought to accept salvation mainly through the influence of early training. Though parents should aim at nothing short of the early conversion of their child, by means of a perfect discipline, and though they should not expect, (as I fear many do,) that he will be saved merely because he is "a child of the covenant," has been baptised, and received some religious instruction, yet they may hope for his salvation in proportion as they have been faithful in training him for God. It is found that very aged people remember the events of their childhood much more readily and distinctly than those of later life.[41] There is hope, then, that what was taught them at the fireside, will be recollected by them even in their old age, and be the means of their salvation. Instances of the kind have sometimes occurred. And they would more frequently occur, if aged sinners were oftener reminded of their early religious training.[42]

The other encouragement is, that, whether converted in childhood or in more advanced life, they will be the more stable, consistent, and useful Christians, in proportion to the thoroughness of their early religious training. If they are converted young, it will be all the better in this respect. Nevertheless, if they are not converted till middle life or old age even, the restraints and instructions of their childhood will be no little aid to them in living a correct religious life. Such are found, therefore, to be most persevering, stable, and uniform. Rev. Jacob Little, of Granville, Ohio, reports that of four hundred and three of the members of his church who were baptized in infancy, only seventeen had been excommunicated, while out of one hundred and fifty-seven who were baptized in adult years, twenty-one had been excommunicated; that is, only about one in twenty-four of the former went astray, while one in six and a half of the others went astray. And this difference could not have been occasioned by the difference of the ages at which they were baptized, but by the difference of their early training. The former were baptised in infancy because they were the children of pious parents, who strove, consequently, to "bring them up in the nurture and admonition of the Lord." And this early training it was that made them so correct and consistent as professors of religion.

We see on the whole, then, that parents have ample encouragement to be faithful in their efforts to "train up their children in the way they should go;" since the more judicious and thorough they are, the greater is the probability that these children will be converted—will become the more correct, and useful, and happy in life, and will reap the richer reward in heaven. Yes; and at the same time we see most powerful considerations to deter them from neglect of parental duty, which is too prevalent among those who profess to be blessed by "faith with faithful Abraham." For, to them are committed souls which "worlds want wealth to buy" — souls whose salvation they might secure if they would be sufficiently faithful as to influence, authority, and instruction. What a crushing responsibility, then, is resting upon them. How great, therefore, must be their guilt, and how great should be their grief, if they suffer them to perish. Oh, if the generality of parents were as mindful as they should be of their awful accountability as to the final destiny of their children, they would not, they could not, so grievously neglect their moral and religious training.

Would to God, that all those on whom this responsibility is resting, would lay this subject suitably to heart; and would firmly resolve to labor for the salvation of their offspring, as they will wish they had, when they come to meet them at the final bar of God!

Psalms cxliv. 12.

*"That our sons may be as plants, grown
up in their youth; that our daughters may
be as corner stones, polished after the
similitude of a palace."*

Lecture 9

The Results of Right Parental Training

*T*he home was once a far more dear and sacred spot; for "modern progress" has despoiled it of much of its former interest and sanctity. Real progress is not to be despised. But in our eager chase after improvements, we should be careful not to leave behind what is more precious than those things after which we are reaching. This caution is doubly needful as regards the good things of home. In the modern increase of our enterprises of pleasure, ambition, and gain, and in the increased facility of travel, we are living more than formerly abroad, and are thereby proportionably weaned from the domestic hearth. And on our return, the multiplication of our occupations and amusements increases yet more our forgetfulness of the family circle. In consequence of these things, the interests and pleasures of the fireside are sadly undervalued and neglected. Yet, nothing left us from the ruins of the fall, is more important to our welfare than a well regulated, happy home. Its archetype is Eden. Its antitype is heaven. No other place on earth, not even the house of God, should be so dear to us. For there our most important duties should be done, and there our richest pleasures enjoyed.

Home, such as it should be, is in part described in the words of our text. The description relates to its most important elements, its dearest inmates. In the preceding verse, the psalmist prays to be delivered from evil children, and in the text, to be blessed with those that are good; or sons that shall "be as plants grown up in their youth," and "daughters like corner stones, polished after the similitude of a palace."

This language is figurative. What, then, is its meaning? The "plants" here mentioned are evidently the same as the "olive plants round about the table," as mentioned by the same writer and for the same purpose, in the 128th psalm. By their "growing up in their youth," we may understand that they had a vigorous growth, not a stinted, gnarly one, as of "a root out of dry ground," having "no form or comeliness;" also, that they had an early maturity. And a flourishing olive, called by the prophet, "a green olive tree, fair, and of goodly fruit," must have been comely on account both of its foliage and fruit. So, in the eye of his affectionate parents, few things are more pleasing than the blooming face and graceful form of a vigorous youth. But the psalmist must have had regard mainly to moral comeliness. And personal beauty is a poor substitute for moral worth. Well, then, may parents be gratified on seeing their sons ripening in all the virtues which qualify them for the domestic and social, the moral and religious activities of life.

But a sentiment prevails among many, that though man was formed for activity, woman was formed only for ornament—not (as the bible teaches) for the "help" of man, but for his admiration and pride; a notion supposed to be confirmed by the fact, that she has more beauty and less strength than man. And how many are led by this notion to educate their daughters to be "beautiful insipidities;" and to regard it as degrading to them to have any useful occupation. But the error is evident. Though man has not the same charms as woman, he has a comeliness as attractive to her, as her beauty is to him. And though she has not his brawny frame, she has equally important duties to perform and is as well fitted by nature for her station, as man is for his. The text speaks, therefore, not only of her beauty, in that she is "polished after the similitude of a palace;" but of her important and powerful position, in that she is a corner stone, thus holding the walls of a vast edifice together.

Woman has been egregiously wronged in being regarded as inferior to man; indeed, among some nations as his drudge, and even his slave; also, in being denied those means of improvement by which she might rise to her proper elevation. Yet, in many instances, she has been wronging herself by failing to improve her mind as much as she might. But of late, if I mistake not, she is in danger of injuring herself in a very different way. It is by overleaping her just claims, and insisting upon occupying a place in society which God has not assigned her, either in creation or revelation. How unwise in her to suppose, that as in a few rare instances she has possessed an energy equal to the more laborious and difficult concerns of life, therefore, all her sex should engage in them, as much as the other sex does now; or to infer from the few instances in which woman of old was called of God to prophecy and to guide the affairs of church and state, that all the sex should share as much as men do in all public labors, civil and religious. It is making that most egregious mistake of putting the *exception* in the place of the *general rule.*

Woman should be found now, where she was generally found under the government of God of old; found where Sarah was, in the retirement of the tent, and where the wives of the Priests and Levites were, at home, not ministering at the altar; found where the virtuous woman mentioned by Solomon was found, "giving meat to her household," "reaching forth her hands to the needy," and "looking well to the ways of her household "—not "sitting among the elders of the land;" found where those women who followed Christ and his apostles were found—not preaching in the temple or synagogues, but ministering to those who did preach there. Women are required of God to "guide the house," not the *church or state;* to be "keepers at home," not *circuit-riders.* Where are women commanded to "preach the word," and to "rule with diligence?" And if it were usually her duty or privilege to do so, how could an inspired apostle have been permitted to say, "Let your women keep silence, for it is not permitted unto them to speak, but they are commanded to be under obedience, as also saith the law. And if they will learn anything, let them ask their husbands at home, [not *teach* them in the house of God,] for it is a shame for a woman to speak in the church."[43] And how could he have been permitted to say again, "Let your women learn in silence, with all subjection. But I suffer not a woman to teach, nor to usurp authority over the man; but to be in silence."[44] And if she should not be conspicuously active in the church, she should not in any other concourse that is equally public.

When woman insists on taking the place of man in society, it is as if the hind wheel of a carriage should claim to run on the fore axletree. So long as she keeps within her proper sphere, her activity is important. But if she leaves it, things move badly; and none the better, though she should be the bigger wheel of the two. Novelty, or other excitements, may give the vehicle at first an additional velocity. But as it moves by morbid action, it cannot move safely.

And in such a course, woman must injure herself, as well as the cause in which she engages. Although many for a while may admire her blowzy cheek and Bloomer costume, her silver voice and her impassioned language, still unintoxicated, plain, common sense will decide with Paul, that "it is a shame for a woman to speak" in public —that by thus unsexing herself she does herself a serious dishonor. And it is evident that all the reforms of the day in which she has taken a public part, have suffered discredit and injury thereby.

But the worse thing in this movement is, that it smells of *infidelity*. Although some females who engage in this crusade for "Woman's Rights" are putting on the livery of Christ and are even professing to preach the gospel, they must be "wolves in sheep's clothing," or at least are sadly deluded. For they grievously contravene the rules of Christ's house. Christianity needs the labors of female preachers now, no more than it needed the testimony of that damsel who "brought her masters much gain by soothsaying;" and who followed Paul and his companions saying, "These men are the servants of the most high God, which show unto us the way of salvation."[45] A great share of the advocates of what are called "woman's rights "are semi-infidels, if not avowedly infidels in full. But how preposterous in them to trample on Christianity, which has done more than all things else to elevate woman to her proper place among men.

Far be it from me to intimate that a great share of the softer sex are enlisted in this movement. I believe, rather, that its advocates are comparatively few. These have been called, either ironically or otherwise, "our strong-minded women." But I think they might be more appropriately styled "our *strong-hearted* women." And some of them are so masculine, that their desire for manly stations and manly employments is not so much to be wondered at. Whereas, by far the greater share of the sisterhood, comprising those of the most mental and moral worth, are fully persuaded that woman's appropriate place is not in camp or cabinet, workshop or plow-field; neither in the pulpit, at the bar; or on the platform, but in the family and the social circles; and that she has most loveliness and worth, when her eye beams most with benevolence, and her hands abound most in good works.

The model of an excellent family, as graphically though briefly described in the text, is one in which all the children, male and female, are "trained up in the way they should go;" and thus, are furnished for all the purposes of life, their wills being subdued, their dispositions rendered sweet and affectionate, their minds fully instructed as to their domestic, social, and religious duties, and their habits formed and fixed accordingly. In such a family, the reigning spirits are love to parents, brothers and sisters, and good will to all.

Such a family is a rich blessing to its *parents, to its children* and to the *community*. To its parents it is a blessed retreat from the evils which they see or feel abroad. As the worthy mother returns home, sated and sickened with what she has seen of extravagance in dress, furniture, and equipage, how welcome must be her own neat and quiet domicile. As she comes back, disgusted with the empty etiquette and the heartless professions of a false and fashionable world, how happy she is to find herself surrounded with those dear ones whose warm expressions of affection she knows to be sincere. And how much are those mothers to be pitied, who never had a love for these enjoyments of home; or who have lost it among the frivolities and intoxications of fashionable life. And how much more are those to be pitied, who have never provided such enjoyments; who, therefore, on returning home, are met by a clamorous and contentious household, and whose hearts are grieved, if not exasperated, at the manner in which their children treat themselves and each other.

So also of the father. As he returns from his daily employment, worn down by its toils, oppressed by its cares, and perplexed, perhaps, by its incidental disasters, how cheering to meet at home an affectionate, buoyant, happy family of sons and daughters. What a blessing to have one place of quiet and confidence in this tumultuous and false-hearted world. If he meet with hard-heartedness or treachery, abuse or violence, how delightful to think of one company of affectionate and confiding ones, whose every profession is true, and whose every action is kind and sympathizing. And if he be ever so prosperous, his home should be his dearest object. For, in no pomp or pleasure, and in no thought of wealth or honor, can he find so much satisfaction as in the bosom of his well trained and lovely family. How unwise, then, the father who gets so absorbed in things abroad, as to lose his interest in the heaven-appointed enjoyments of home. Especially how unwise, if he fails to do his part toward "bringing up his children in the nurture and admonition of the Lord," thus failing of the enjoyments just described, and thus entailing on himself a family, selfish and unkind, discordant and contentious, consequently, a source of perplexity and pain to him.

Thus important is a well trained family to parents. But it is much more so to children. For, in the first place, they will be far more happy for it. To see this, you have only to compare them with such as have not been governed and instructed as they ought to be. In ill-governed and untaught families, you will see let loose all those passions by which children torture themselves and each other. All is insubordination and impatience, contention and wrath. The younger are crying from vexation; the elder contending and threatening, if not battling with one another. And how much more unhappy must such a household be, than one where all is peace, and harmony and love.

How cruel those parents, then, who neglect to train their children to walk in the ways of pleasantness, and the paths of peace. By allowing the child to indulge his anger for the hour together, they allow him, in fact, to inflict upon himself an hour of distress and pain. And by allowing him thus to form the habit of impatience and revenge, they prepare him for far more of these self-inflicted sufferings. And while tormenting himself, he is tormenting his fellows. Who can estimate the evil, then, of bringing up a whole family to be thus "hateful and hating one another." How much more happy must that family be, where, from the youngest to the eldest, all are "loving one another with a pure heart, fervently," and are taking great satisfaction in seeing and in making each other happy. Such are some Christian families, and such should all of them be.

And in the next place, the sons and daughters, rightly trained, will be the better qualified to do the duties of fathers and mothers in families of their own. They will know the better how to govern and instruct them. Having been so long accustomed to the good methods of their parents, it will be the more natural to adopt, and the more easy to practice them.

Custom has usually a sad and powerful influence over those whose training has been bad. They generally bring up their own children as they have been brought up themselves. Sometimes, however, they see and deplore the errors of their parents, and resolve to bring up their own children differently. Yet, though they begin well, they are apt shortly to slide into those habits of their parents which they previously deplored. This is one of the ways in which God is visiting the iniquities of the fathers upon their children unto the third and fourth generation. Whereas, if they would train their children correctly, they probably, through the influence of habit and the true promised grace of God, would send a rich blessing far down the line of their own posterity.

Finally, a well trained family is a rich blessing to the *state* and the *church.* It furnishes our most useful citizens and our most faithful saints. Those who have been most obedient to their parents, will be most submissive to laws of their country and their God. And those who have been best instructed at the fireside, will generally be most thoroughly taught the morality and religion of the bible—that is, to love God supremely, and their neighbor as themselves; taught, therefore, to practice on those principles of benevolence, liberty, and justice, which the word of God inculcates. And those who are so early and thoroughly imbued with such principles, will be the last to *sway others,* and the last *themselves to swerve* from political rectitude. These are the ones, therefore, that we need for the coming strife, when Europe shall have poured to the utmost, her ignorant and dangerous population upon us; the ones that will then be needed to watch our polls, to fill our jury boxes, and to guard and execute our laws.

Nor let it be supposed that the daughters of America have nothing to do toward saving and blessing their country. While they should not be heard in the caucus or on the platform, yet in the family and in the social circles, their persuasions may avail much. In this respect, their relation to the other sex is like that of the legal counselor to the public advocate. The former gives that advice in the law-chamber which the latter employs in the public hall. And many is the man who has received a wise and timely suggestion, check, or impulse, from a mother, sister, or wife. Many a man has been heard to say, "If I had heeded my wife, it would have saved me from ruin." Yes, well did the wisest of kings say, — "The price of a virtuous woman is above rubies. The heart of her husband doth safely trust in her, so that he shall have no need of spoils. Her husband is known in the gates, when he sitteth among the rulers of the land."[46] It is true, that the suggestions of woman have sometimes been deplorable. But from her who tempted Adam to take the forbidden fruit, and from her who urged Job to "curse God and die," and from her who urged Herod to behead John the Baptist, let us turn away to the myriads of women whose warm hearts and persuasive lips are ever on the side of virtue and injured humanity. And such, probably, will all those be, who are truly "brought up in the nurture and admonition of the Lord." In short, I know of nothing more important to our political welfare, than to have all families led early by their parents "in the way they should go."

And equally important is such parental training to the welfare of the church and the salvation of mankind. Religion lies at the foundation of all genuine morality and patriotism. That nurture, then, which best qualifies our sons and daughters for promoting man's social and political welfare, will more directly qualify them to promote his salvation. We have seen, in former discourses, that this nurture is well suited to secure the renewal of the heart, and the instruction of the understanding in the fundamental principles of religion; suited, also, to root and ground them in the practice of these principles, and to secure to them a life of *faithful, uniform,* and *consistent* obedience. And these things prepare them to feel deeply and labor industriously for man's eternal welfare. In the instructions of the Sabbath school, in the distribution of tracts, and in all kindred labors, we find those to be most prompt and persevering who have been most faithfully trained in the nursery and parlor.

But at present the loudest call of the church is, for laborers in the capacity of pastors, missionaries, and teachers, male and female. And where are we to look for them, if not to the families that are "brought up in the nurture and admonition of the Lord?" The way, then, in which parents can do most for Zion, is to train their children for the service of God—to educate them, not as too many do, to self-indulgence and self-will, to frivolity and pleasure, to parade and extravagance, nor to the acquirement of wealth and honor; but to that in which they would find, both now and at last, their greatest delight, and riches, and glory. Oh, if all those parents who profess to have renounced the world, and to have devoted their all to God, would make a sincere offering of their children to him, and would prove their sincerity by actually training them to "serve their own generation by the will of God," what a reformation would be the result. Not only would "many be added to the church" of "such as shall be saved," but a goodly share of them would be preparing to "preach the word." And soon would many of these be ready to labor in the gospel field, not only at home, but in "the ends of the earth."

Nor would she who was "last at the cross, and first at the sepulchre," be lingering in this great work. Though she is required to "keep silence in the churches," yet, like Priscilla, she can aid an eloquent Apollos, by "expounding unto him the way of God more perfectly;"[47] and by various suggestions and encouragements can greatly increase his usefulness. Much more can she accomplish by instructing in families and schools, and in efforts to raise the needful funds to send the gospel to the destitute.

As, then, the well-trained family conduces so much to the happiness of parents and children, and so much to the political and spiritual welfare of others, we see ample reasons why David should pray, in the text, that all the families of Israel should be such. We see ample reasons, also, why Christian parents should strive to the utmost to bring up their children as God has directed them in his holy word. Would to God all of them might be so faithful in doing it, as to secure all the happy results that have been dwelt upon in the foregoing discourses.

Appendix

AFTER preparing the foregoing lectures, I was led to read in Tupper's *Proverbial Philosophy* an article entitled "Education". And in that article I was pleased to find many pithy sentences fully coinciding with several important positions which I have taken in these lectures. I therefore append some of the more apposite of them, in hopes that they will not only confirm my opinions, but fix them more firmly, in the reader's memory.

As far as I could, I have arranged these quotations so as to correspond with the order in which their subjects are treated on in the previous lectures.

LECTURE 1.

PARENTAL TRAINING.

A babe in a house is a well-spring of pleasure, a messenger of
    peace and love

A resting place for innocence on earth; a link between angels and
    men:

Yet is it a talent of trust, a loan to be rendered back with interest;

A delight, but redolent with care; a honey-sweet, but lacking not
    the bitter.

For character groweth day by day, and all things aid it in
    unfolding.

And the bent unto good or evil may be given in the hours of
    infancy.

Select not to nurse thy darling one that may taint his innocence,

For example is a constant monitor, and good seed will die among
    the tares.

The arts of a strange servant have spoiled a gentle disposition

Mother, let him learn of thy lips, and be nourished at thy breast.

Character is mainly molded by the cast of minds that surround it

Let then the playmates of thy little one be not other than thy judgment shall approve.

LECTURE 2.
PARENTAL INFLUENCE.
For disposition is builded up by the fashionings of *first impressions*
Wherefore, though the voice of Instruction waiteth for the ear of
reason,
Yet with the mother's milk the young child drinketh Education.
Patience is the first lesson: he may learn it at the breast:
And the habit of obedience and trust may be grafted on his mind
in the cradle.
Lo, thou art a land-mark on a hill; thy little ones copy thee in all
things
Let, then, thy religion be perfect: so shalt thou be honored in thy
house.

LECTURE 3.
PARENTAL AUTHORITY.
Show me a child undutiful, and I shall know where to look for a
foolish father
Never hath a father done his duty, and lived to be despised of his
son.
But how can that son reverence an example he dare not follow?
Should he imitate thee in thine evil? his scorn is thy rebuke.
Nay, but bring him up aright, in obedience to God and to thee.

LECTURE 4.
PARENTAL AUTHORITY.
Above all things graft on him subjection, yea in the veriest trifle:
Courtesy to all, reverence to some, and to thee unanswering
obedience.
...

Begin betimes, lest thou fail of his fear, and with judgment that
   thou lose not his love.

...

Be obeyed when thou commandest; but command not often

...

A mild rebuke in the season of calmness is better than a rod in the
   heat of passion,

Nevertheless spare not, if thy word hath passed for punishment;

Let not thy child see thee humbled, nor learn to think thee false.

LECTURE 5.

GOVERNMENT IN LOVE.

Let thy carriage be the gentleness of love, not the stern front of
   tyranny.

Suffer none to reprove thee before him, and reprove not thine
   own purposes by change;

Yet speedily turn again, and reward him where thou canst,

For kind encouragement in good cutteth at the roots of evil.

When his reason yieldeth fruit, make thy child thy friend:

For a filial friend is a double gain, a diamond set in gold.

As an infant, thy mandate was enough, but now let him see thy
   reasons;

Confide in him, but with discretion: and bend a willing ear to his
   questions.

More to thee than to all beside, let him owe good counsel and
   good guidance;

Let him feel his pursuits have an interest more to thee than to all
   beside.

LECTURE 6.

PARENTAL INSTRUCTION.

For a child is in a new world and learneth somewhat every
   moment

His eye is quick to observe, his memory storeth in secret,

His ear is greedy of knowledge, and his mind plastic as soft wax.

Beware, then, that he heareth what is good, that he feed not on evil maxims.

For the seeds of first instructions are dropped into the deepest furrows.

That which immemorial use hath sanctioned, seemeth to be right and true;

Therefore, let him never have to recollect the time when good things were strangers to his thoughts.

...

Read thou first, and well approve, the books thou givest thy child;

But remember the weakness of his thought, and that wisdom for him must be diluted

In honied waters of infant tales, let him taste the strong wine of truth

Pathetic stories soften the heart; but the legends of terror breed midnight misery

Fairy fictions cram the mind with folly, and knowledge of evil tempteth to like evil.

...

The mind is made wealthy by ideas, but the multitude of words is a clogging weight:

Therefore be understood in thy teaching, and instruct to the measure of capacity.

Analogy is milk for babes, but abstract truths are strong meat;

Precepts and rules are repulsive to a child, but happy illustration winneth him.

Things undefined are full of dread, and stagger stouter nerves.

The seeds of misery and madness have been sowed in the nights of infancy;

Therefore be careful that ghastly fears be not the night companions of thy child.

LECTURE 7.

PARENTAL MISMANAGEMENT.

Finding nothing in Proverbial Philosophy on the subjects of this lecture, I would refer the reader to T. S. Arthur's "Iron Rule," to Anderson's "Book for Parents," pp. 232–3, and to "Anecdotes for the Family Circle," pp. 138, 158. But of the "Iron Rule" I must say, it has some serious faults. It rightly condemns Mr. Howland for imposing unreasonable restraints on his son, for refusing to let him justify himself, and for punishing him with too much sternness and too little affection. But it is wrong in intimating that these faults were the *only* cause of his failing to secure his child's obedience. The main cause of the failure was, that he did not *begin in season* to govern him. He should have begun in the *first* instead of the *seventh* year. The task of securing complete obedience should be mainly, if not entirely, accomplished before the child is two years old. And this is the greatest fault of most parents, and of many writers on parental government, that they do not insist on this early enforcement of obedience.

Another fault of the book is, that it evidently intimates that parents should not insist on being obeyed in *all things*. And thus it contradicts Dr. Witherspoon, who insists that parental authority should be "entire and absolute;" and Tupper, who says, "Above all things, graft on him subjection, yea in the veriest trifle . . . Be obeyed when thou commandest; but command not often."

Thus, it fails to enforce, and virtually discourages that *early* and *entire* obedience which it is easiest for the parent to secure and for the child to yield, and which, therefore, would save a great amount of severity and suffering.

LECTURE 0.

PARENTAL ENCOURAGEMENT.

Hold the little hands in prayer, teach the weak knees their
    kneeling;

Let him see thee speaking to thy God; he will not forget it
  afterward

When old and gray, will he feelingly remember a mother's tender
  piety,

And the touching recollection of her prayers shall arrest the strong
  man in his sin.

And if thou train him to trust thee, he will not withhold his reli-
  ance from the Lord.

Notes

1   See Deut. vii. 9.

2   Deut. v. 29.

3   Gen. xii. 3.

4   See Gen. xvii. 7, and Psalm lxxviii. 5, 6.

5   Ex. xx. 12; Prov. i. 8; vi. 20; xxx. 17.

6   The terms, "godfathers" and "godmothers," are to me almost profane and revolting, as there is so little of God's authority in their appointment, and, often, so little of the Spirit of God in themselves.

7   See Rev. Jacob Little's Report, 1855.

8   But the measure here recommended is not to be confounded with a hurtful one used by some parents—that of checking and crossing their children after they are two years old and upward, for the avowed purpose of breaking their wills, and of making it easier for them to practice self-denial. The effort must be commenced before they are a year old, and be made in love with firmness, or it will be worse than useless. Concerning these later efforts, a poet has said:
> "He who checks a child with terror,
>   Stops its play and stills its song,
> Not alone commits an error,
>   But a grievous moral wrong.
> Give it play, and never fear it;
>   Active life is no defect;
> Never, never break its spirit;
>   Curb it only to direct.
> Would you stop the flowing river,
>   Thinking it would cease to flow
> Onward it must flow forever;
>   Better teach it where to go."

9   2 Sam. vii. 14; Job, ix. 34; xxi. 9; Ps. lxxxix. 32; Prov. x. 13; xiii. 24; xxii. 15; xxiii. 13, 14; xxvi. 3; xxix. 15; 1 Cor. iv. 21.

10   2 Sam. vii. 14; Ps. lxxxix. 32; Prov. xiii. 24; xvii. 10; xix. 18, 29; xx. 30; Luke, xii. 47, 48; Heb, xii. 5–8.

11   See Note under the Eighth Discourse.

12   1 Sam. iii. 13.

13   Ex. xx. 12.

14   Mal. i 6.

15   Ps. xxxix 9.

16   Mat. xi. 26.

17   Rom. ix. 20.

18   In subduing the will of an obstinate child, the firmness of many mothers is put to a severe trial. And she is in danger of giving over the attempt, and of thus ruining her child. For the encouragement of such, I give the following extract from a letter written me by a lady, while I was preparing this work. The whole letter would be interesting, but it is too long for insertion here. After giving a glowing account of her adopted daughter's lovely conduct on a certain Sabbath morning, she adds "That little child, which, only two hours before, had seemed as pure and holy as an angel, was now a 'very thing of madness.' The waters had been stirred—her will opposed; and she, for the first time in her life, refused to obey. One hour rolled away, and kind entreaties, and gentle words, and plain reasoning availed nothing. 'I must of necessity resort to the remedy which Solomon in his wisdom recommended.' This seemed only to infuriate; and had it not been for the encouragement of an aged Christian friend present, one whose judgment could be relied upon, I fear my task would have been too much for me. My own position, at this time, was painfully critical, from the fact that this little charge was the dying legacy of a sainted sister. Firmness and duty to God and my child were all-important, then, as the future would be marked by that hour. After giving her sufficient time to say and feel that she was 'sorry, and that she loved mamma,' I found her lost to all penitence. She would toss herself to and fro upon the bed, where I had placed her, that she might not tire herself out by efforts and outcries. Frequently did I turn to my friend, and in anguish ask, 'What shall I do?' His answer was, 'Persevere; if you do not, you will reap sorrow for your child.

Break her will, or she will break your heart.' Then, with uplifted heart, in strong desire for wisdom from on high, and in the feeling that the spirit of my departed sister was hovering around that scene, I endeavored to go forward in the way of my duty. Messages were sent from all parts of the house [a large hotel] that I was cruelly severe; that I would ruin her disposition; cause her to 'hate' me—friends and servants even intruded upon my presence — but I was calm and unmoved, and asked them to leave; the responsibility was my own, and I believed God would bless the result. Another hour rolled away, and language, and tears, and stripes were in vain. 'I do not feel sorry; I do not love mamma,' was still reiterated. I really apprehended danger to her mental and physical powers; and the fear was fast taking possession of my mind, that she would not yield. Again was a silent prayer put up. Then, while a look of pity and anguish was cast upon my little sufferer, she looked me intently, for a moment, in the eye, and rushed into my arms, reiterating, 'I do feel sorry; I will be a good girl. I love God, and mamma, too.' She sank upon my bosom, covering me with kisses, and dropped to sleep.

"It being suggested by someone that she would turn away from her mother upon waking, my husband put this suggestion to the test. Placing ourselves by her bedside, when she awakened, she gave her usually sweet smile to both of us; then reached out her little hands for mother to please take her up, and inquired if she could go to church after dinner, if she was a good child? Since that period, we have never required anything but what has been cheerfully and immediately granted. Once speaking, with firmness, has been and is enough to command immediate obedience. And whoever knows little Addie S. will say more in praise of her loveliness than is befitting a mother. I have now told my painful story, in hopes it may be the means of aiding some mother in her duty to the little immortals committed to her love."

19   Heb. xii. 6; Rev. iii. 19.
20   Lam. iii. 33; Heb. xii. 10.

21   It has been told in praise of a certain mother, that when requested
     to order her children away from certain mischief, she said to them,
     "The child who loves his mother best, will come right to her." The
     consequence was, that every child forsook his mischief, and rushed
     to his mother's side. This was indeed better than harshly scolding,
     or beating them away from it, as many would have done. And yet this
     is not exactly what was needed to be done. There was no obedience
     on the part of the children, for there was no command on the part
     of the mother. They did not leave their mischief (as children should
     be made to do) out of regard to the authority of the parent, but out
     of emulation. Each one wished to have the credit of "loving mother
     best."

22   In confirmation of this, see "Mother at Home," pp. 123-4, and "Infant
     Philosophy," p. 210.

23   1 Tim. iii. 15.

24   Prov. xix. 18.

25   See "Infant Philosophy," pp. 80-2 and 197-8.

26   See "Mother at Home," pp. 113-14.

27   Tit. iii. 5.

28   1 Pet. i. 22.

29   Eph. vi. 4.

30   Gen. xviii. 19.

31   See Ps. lxxviii. 5-7.

32   Prov. xxii. 15; xxiii. 13, 15; xxix. 15, 17.

33   Mark, x, 15.

34   A letter written by a very intelligent and pious mother of my acquain-
     tance, who has gone to her rest, has somehow fallen into my hands.
     As a portion of it is very appropriate to the subject before us, I feel
     constrained to quote it. She says:
        "Many of my friends have heard me relate the circumstances
     attending the hopeful conversion of each of my children; but as the
     rod was concerned in one case only, it is not necessary here to men-
     tion the others. The facts in that case being simply the following,

speak for themselves. In consequence of repeated acts of disobedience, and one or two of falsehood, and after more lenient measures
had been often used, I was satisfied that duty required me to chastise
my child. As I believed it was not right to use the rod without accom-
panying prayer, knowing that it could do no good without the blessing of God, I took it, with her, to my closet. There, after reading to her
several portions of scripture, where any duty to her as a parent was
enjoined and which she acknowledged, and after we had both im-
portunately entreated the Lord for his assistance and blessing, I
applied the rod once severely. To my grateful astonishment, I soon
found that she was not only bowed in sweet submission to my authority, but that God heard prayer, and was pleased at the same time
to subdue her will to his own. The result was so new to me, that even
while I hoped, I did not venture to speak of it to any individual for
many days. Three or four days elapsed before my daughter indulged
for herself the hope that her sins were forgiven; but the change was
so great and so apparent, I thought I could not be mistaken. Her sub-
sequent life has testified that I was not. At a meeting of the Maternal
Association, some weeks after, I felt that I ought to acknowledge what
the Lord had wrought for my beloved child, and related the circumstances. As this was the first ease of the kind I had ever known or
heard of, it opened before me, in a new and striking light, the imperious duty lying upon parents to subdue the wills of their children to
parental authority, in obedience to plain scriptural commands, with
the humble expectation that God will bless the means of his own
appointment, and enable there to bow their hearts to himself. My
bible lays down the following rules: " Withhold not correction from
a child; for if thou beatest him with the rod, he shall not die. Thou
shalt beat him with the rod, and shalt deliver his soul from hell."
(Prov. xxiii. 13, 14.) Did not Solomon, then, consider the rod as an
appointed means of salvation; that is, if 'deliver,' in the last clause,
means 'save?' James says, 'He that converteth a sinner from the error
of his way shall save a soul from death.' How does 'save a soul from

death' in this passage differ from 'deliver a soul from hell,' in the other? For one, I believe the devil himself has brought the rod into disrepute; and he can take no surer method to regain the dominion of this world, than by frightening parents from the right use of it, when he can succeed in loading it with derision and ignominy, or make mothers love the bodies more than the souls of their children . . .

" . . . An old lady of my acquaintance who was, when a very little child, converted by a blessing on the same means, but which she had been careful not to mention, except to confiding friends, spoke of it, however, on her dying bed, with gratitude to God and her mother too. She even sent for a friend, related the particulars, and requested her to publish them."

Another instance of early conversion under the rod, was related to me by a very judicious and devoted mother, who is still living. She took the same course with the above writer. Before proceeding to punish her little daughter, she took her to the closet, admonished her solemnly and tenderly as to her fault, and the necessity of chastising her, and prayed with her for the blessing of God on the painful duty. After giving her only a few stripes, the child was subdued, and appeared ever after to have a new and Christian spirit. I could mention yet another case of the kind. And I believe, if the application of the rod were generally preceded by admonition and prayer, the like cases of conversion would be much more frequent.

35   Isa. xlv. 19.
36   Gen. xxviii. 14.
37   Gen. xviii. 19.
38   Gen. xvii. 7; Gal. iii. 8, 9.
39   Deut. v. 29; xii. 28; Ps. ciii. 17; Prov. xx. 7.
40   Prov. xxii. 15; xxiii. 13, 14; xxix. 17.
41   Luke Short was converted by means of a sermon of Flavel's, recollected eighty-five years after he heard it. Christian Family Almanac, 1855.

42   See Infant Philosophy, pp. 258–261.

43   1 Cor. xiv. 34, 35.

44   1 Tim. ii. 11, 12.

45   Acts, xvi. 16, 17.

46   Prov. xxxi. 10, 11, 23.

47   Acts, xviii. 26.

Index

References to endnotes are listed first by the page number in the *Notes* section, then followed in parentheses by the page number of the location of that endnote in the text.

www.ingramcontent.com/pod-product-compliance
Lightning Source LLC
Chambersburg PA
CBHW020516100426
42813CB00030B/3272/J